Canada's Lar

Grades 4-6

Written by Ruth Solski
Illustrated by Ric Ward

ISBN 1-55035-727-1
Canada's Landmarks, SSJ1-48

Revised Feb. 2003
15 Dairy Avenue
Napanee, Ontario
K7R 1M4

A Division of the Solski Group

 "We acknowledge the financial support of the Government of Canada through the Book Publishing Industry Development program for our publishing activities."

Published in Canada by:
S&S Learning Materials
15 Dairy Avenue
Napanee, Ontario
K7R 1M4
www.sslearning.com

Published in the United States by:
T4T Learning Materials
3909 Witmer Road PMB 175
Niagara Falls, New York
14305
www.t4tlearning.com

Look For

Other Canadian Units

Item #SSJ1-01 Canada .... Gr. 1
J1-02 All About Canada 2
J1-03 Let's Visit Canada 3
J1-04 Canadian Provinces 3-6
J1-11 Wild Animals of Canada 2-3
J1-12 Famous Canadians 4-8
J1-13 Let's Look at Canada 4-6
J1-23 Ottawa 7-9
J1-32 What is Canada? .... P-K
J1-33 Canadian Capital Cities 4-6
J1-35 Toronto 4-8
J1-37 Canadian Arctic Inuit 2-3
J1-38 Canadian Provinces and Territories 4-6
J1-39 Canadian Government 5-8
J1-40 Development of Western Canada 7-8
J1-41 Canada and Its Trading Partners 6-8
J1-42 Canada's Traditions and Celebrations 1-3
J1-45 Fathers of Confederation 4-8
J1-47 Prime Ministers of Canada 4-8
J1-48 Canada's Landmarks 4-6

Let's Visit...

J1-14 Let's Visit Saskatchewan 2-4
J1-15 Let's Visit British Columbia 2-4
J1-16 Let's Visit Alberta 2-4
J1-17 Let's Visit Ontario 2-4
J1-18 Let's Visit Manitoba 2-4
J1-19 Let's Visit Prince Edward Island 2-4
J1-20 Let's Visit Nova Scotia 2-4
J1-21 Let's Visit New Brunswick 2-4
J1-27 Let's Visit Newfoundland and Labrador 2-4
J1-28 Let's Visit Yukon Territory 2-4
J1-30 Let's Visit Northwest Territory 2-4
J1-31 Let's Visit Québec 2-4
J1-34 Let's Visit Nunavut 2-4

Discover Canada

J1-22 Discover Québec 5-7
J1-24 Discover Prince Edward Island 5-7
J1-25 Discover Ontario 5-7
J1-26 Discover Nova Scotia 5-7
J1-36 Discover Nunavut Territory 5-7

Canadian Communities

J1-05 Farming Community 3-4
J1-06 Fishing Community 3-4
J1-07 Mining Community 3-4
J1-08 Lumbering Community 3-4
J1-09 Ranching Community 3-4
J1-10 Inuit Community 3-4

Published by:
S&S Learning Materials
15 Dairy Avenue
Napanee, Ontario
K7R 1M4

Distributed in U.S.A. by:
T4T Learning Materials
3909 Witmer Road PMB 175
Niagara Falls, New York
14305

CANADA'S LANDMARKS

Table of Contents

CANADA'S LANDMARKS

Introduction to Teachers

Canada's Landmarks provides information and follow-up activities on various landmarks located in Canada. The main objective of the material in the book is to familiarize and broaden student knowledge with the location and historical aspects of heritage sites found throughout their country. With this knowledge, deeper feelings of pride and patriotism will be fostered.

The information and follow-up exercises may be used to develop reading skills such as: noting details, sequencing, recalling facts and events, vocabulary meanings, context clues and making inferences. Research skills will be enhanced through the implementation of the Internet activities. The open-ended activities may be used to develop student creativity and higher level thinking skills.

The information and activities may be worked on in any order and may be used in the classroom by the teacher in the format that best suits the needs of his/her students.

Canada's Capital Region

Ottawa, Canada's capital, is located on the border of the province of Ontario. It was made the capital of the Province of Canada in 1857 by Queen Victoria. Today, a much larger Capital Region serves as a frame for Canada's capital. The Capital Region consists of Ottawa and Gatineau as well as numerous small towns and rural communities. It covers an area of 4715 square kilometres that stretches out on both sides of the Ottawa River to include parts of two Canadian provinces: Québec to the north and Ontario to the south. The region has a population of 1 081 000 (2000). The Capital Region is one of Canada's most bilingual communities. Nearly half a million people speak both English and French fluently.

Ottawa is a city of national symbols. Its buildings, statues, museums and memorials represent the history and values of Canadians. Visitors take away a deeper understanding of Canada and its people. These symbols also highlight Canada's democracy, provinces and territories, Canadian land-scapes, Canadians in war and peace, Canadian heroes, Canadian achievers and Canada in the world.

Parliament Hill and the **Peace Tower** symbolize Canadian democracy making Canada one of the freest and most peaceful societies in the world. The **Centennial Flame** represents Canada's provinces and territories. It has burned since 1961 and represents Canadian unity. Provincial and territorial flags fly along the length of Confederation Boulevard and in the Garden of Provinces in their honour.

The **National War Memorial** and the **Tomb of the Unknown Soldier** honour Canadians who died in war. Millions of tulips bloom in May in the Capital Region to remind us of the role Canada played helping The Netherlands during World War Two.

Modern and historic heroes are remembered in the Capital as well. Terry Fox, a modern day hero, ran halfway across Canada to raise money for cancer research in 1981. Today, a statue of him running can be seen on Wellington Street. Samuel de Champlain, a hero from the past, was a French explorer who travelled the Ottawa River in 1613 and founded a nation. His statue stands on Nepean Point honouring his efforts and achievements. Statues and monuments can be seen on and around Parliament Hill. They have been erected to honour Prime Ministers, Royalty and Fathers of Confederation.

There are more museums in Ottawa than in any other Canadian city. The **Canadian Museum of Civilization** celebrates the achievements of cultures from the present and the past. Other museums depict the history of Canadian farming, nature, money, air travel, science, technology, art, communication and photography.

Canada's Capital Region is a wonderful place to experience Canadian history, visit national museums, view historic sites and monuments, and to become acquainted with the government and how it works.

Activity **Name:** ____________________

Let's Research Canada's Capital Region!

Using your favourite internet search engine, run a search using the key words "Canada's Capital and Its Region".

At the site, locate information needed to complete the following activities. Record your answers on the lines provided.

1. How many statues are located on Parliament Hill?

   ____

2. List the names of the famous Canadians who have been honoured.

   ____
   ____
   ____
   ____
   ____
   ____

3. Choose one of the statues and find out why the person was recognized for his/her achievements.

   ____
   ____
   ____
   ____

4. How many monuments can you see in the city of Ottawa?

   ____

5. List the names of the monuments and their locations on the following chart.

Monument	Location

Name: ___________________

Ottawa's History Challenge

Ottawa's history has been an eventful one. Over the years, it has changed its face many times and is now the treasure house of Canada's heritage and a meeting place for all Canadians.

Carefully read the following events that took place in Ottawa's history.

Number the events in the order in which they happened:

_____ In 1806, Wright built a raft out of squared timber and floated it down the Ottawa River to Québec City. This proved that logging in the Ottawa Valley was possible.

_____ In the early 1850's, sawmills buzzed noisily, the air was filled with saw dust, lumber was piled high and great fortunes were made from the lumbering industry.

_____ The Parliament Buildings of Canada were completed in 1866, just in time for Confederation which took place in 1867.

_____ The first inhabitants of the Ottawa River Valley were the Algonquin Native People.

_____ Although the north side of the Ottawa River (Wrights Town) hummed with activity in the 1810's and 1820's, the south side of the river was a virtual wilderness.

_____ Since then, the Centre Block has been rebuilt and Ottawa has been transformed into a scenic, green capital city.

_____ Etienne Brulé was the first European to explore the Ottawa River.

_____ In time, the Ottawa Valley was the major timber-producing area in Upper and Lower Canada.

_____ In 1613, Champlain, a French explorer, arrived in what is now the capital and made detailed maps of the Ottawa Region.

_____ In 1826, Lieutenant-Colonel John By changed the south side of the Ottawa River when he and his workers began the construction of the Rideau Canal.

_____ In 1857, Queen Victoria chose Ottawa to be the capital city of the United Province of Canada.

_____ When the Rideau Canal was finished in 1832, many of the workers stayed on in the community called Bytown.

_____ In 1916, the Centre Block on Parliament Hill was destroyed by fire. All that was left standing was the Library of Parliament.

_____ In 1855, the name of Bytown no longer suited the growing town and it was incorporated as the City of Ottawa.

_____ In 1899, Prime Minister Wilfrid Laurier said that Ottawa was not a handsome city so he created the Ottawa Improvement Commission to beautify the parks and to clean up the Ottawa River.

_____ Barracks Hill was chosen as the site, and construction of the Parliament Buildings began in 1860.

_____ The Great Fire of 1900 began in Hull and destroyed lumber mills and nearly two thousand buildings on both sides of the Ottawa River. This changed the face of Canada's capital.

_____ In 1800, Philemon Wright and a group of colonists from Massachusetts settled on the north side of the Ottawa River below Chaudière Falls.

The Parliament Buildings

House of Commons

Canada's **Parliament Buildings** are a distinctive symbol recognized by Canadians and people around the world. Although these buildings come alive with the drama of modern day debates and discussions on a daily basis, the echoes of times and personalities of long ago still linger in the halls and chambers.

The Parliament Buildings stand stately on **Parliament Hill**. The **Centre Block** with its distinctive **Peace Tower** and library is flanked by the **East and West Block**. High vaulted ceilings, marble floors and dramatic lighting create an atmosphere of solemnity inside each building. Their walls bear lively details and decorations.

The **House of Commons** is found at the west end of the **Centre Block**. The **Chamber** is decorated in the traditional green of the British House of Commons. The rectangular chamber is constructed of Canadian white oak and Tyndall limestone from Manitoba. The ceiling is covered with Irish linen that was delicately painted after it was installed. The stained glass windows depict the floral emblems of Canada's provinces and territories and add bold, vibrant colour to this dignified room. A series of sculptures located below the windows explain the parts of Canada's Constitution.

The Senate Foyer

The **Senate Chamber** is located at the east end of the Centre Block. This regal chamber is carpeted and upholstered in red with a ceiling of gold leaf. Hanging from the ceiling are two large bronze chandeliers. The upper walls are covered with murals depicting stirring scenes from World War One. The lower walls bear a frieze showing Canada's plants and animals carved in the Canadian white oak panelling.

The House of Commons and the Senate are separated by **Confederation Hall** and the **Hall of Honour**. Gracefully arched ceilings and detailed sculpture decorate the halls. The **Library of Parliament** is located

Library of parliament

at the end of the Hall of Honour and is a showpiece of neo-gothic architecture. The parquet flooring is made from the wood of oak, cherry and walnut trees. The walls are panelled with Canadian white pine into which have been carved hundreds of flowers, masks, and mythical creatures.

In the centre of the circular, domed room sits an impressive, white marble statue of Queen Victoria. The employees in this library use computer technology to provide information, reference and research services to members of parliament and their staff.

The Peace Tower

Rising above the Parliament Buildings is the well recognized Peace Tower. It was built to celebrate the end of World War One. The tower contains an observation area, a carillon of fifty-three bells and a Memorial Chamber.

The Centre Block also contains many important offices and facilities. The office of the Prime Minister and other party leaders are found in this building.

The East Block houses the restored offices of Canada's first Prime Minister, Sir John A. Macdonald, as well as offices for current parliamentary staff.

The West Block contains committee rooms and offices of members of the House of Commons and is not open to the public.

Name: ____________________

The Parliament Buildings

1. Neatly label the following diagram:

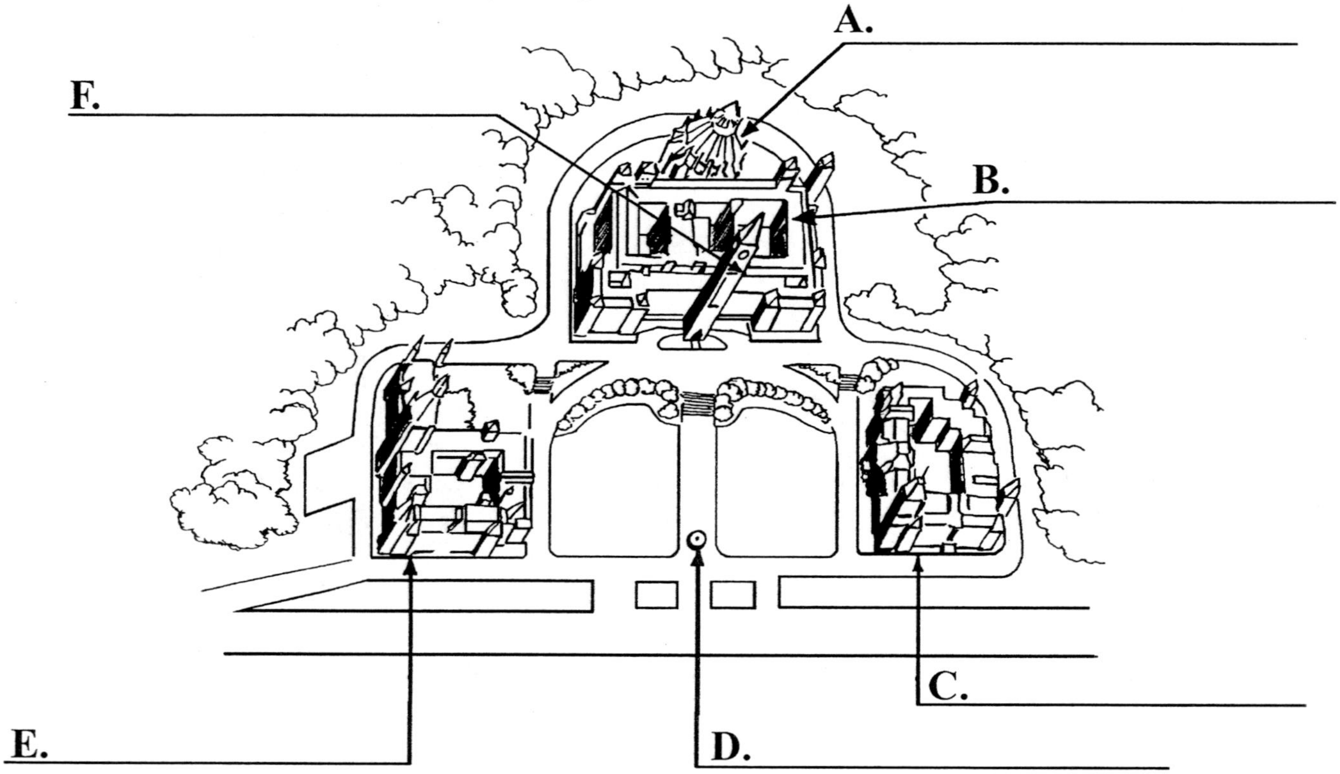

2. The Parliament Buildings are considered a highly recognized symbol of Canada. On the lines provided, record a list of other symbols that represent Canada.

____

____

____

3. Carefully read each group of words. On the line provided, record the location of each item in the Parliament Buildings.

   a) Peace Tower

   ____

   b) Sir John A. Macdonald's office

   ____

   c) committee rooms and offices

   ____

d) Parliamentary Library

____

e) stained glass windows with floral emblems

____

f) red carpet and red upholstered furniture

____

g) the Prime Minister's office

____

h) a frieze of Canadian plants and animals

____

i) a wooden floor made from oak, cherry and walnut trees

____

j) a Carillon of fifty-three bells

____

k) a ceiling covered with Irish linen

____

l) murals on the walls depicting World War One

____

m) a large white marble statue of Queen Victoria

____

4. Using your favourite internet search engine, run a search using the key words "Parliament Buildings of Canada". Read the information to find out more facts and record three new facts on the lines provided.

____

____

____

____

____

____

____

Parliament Hill

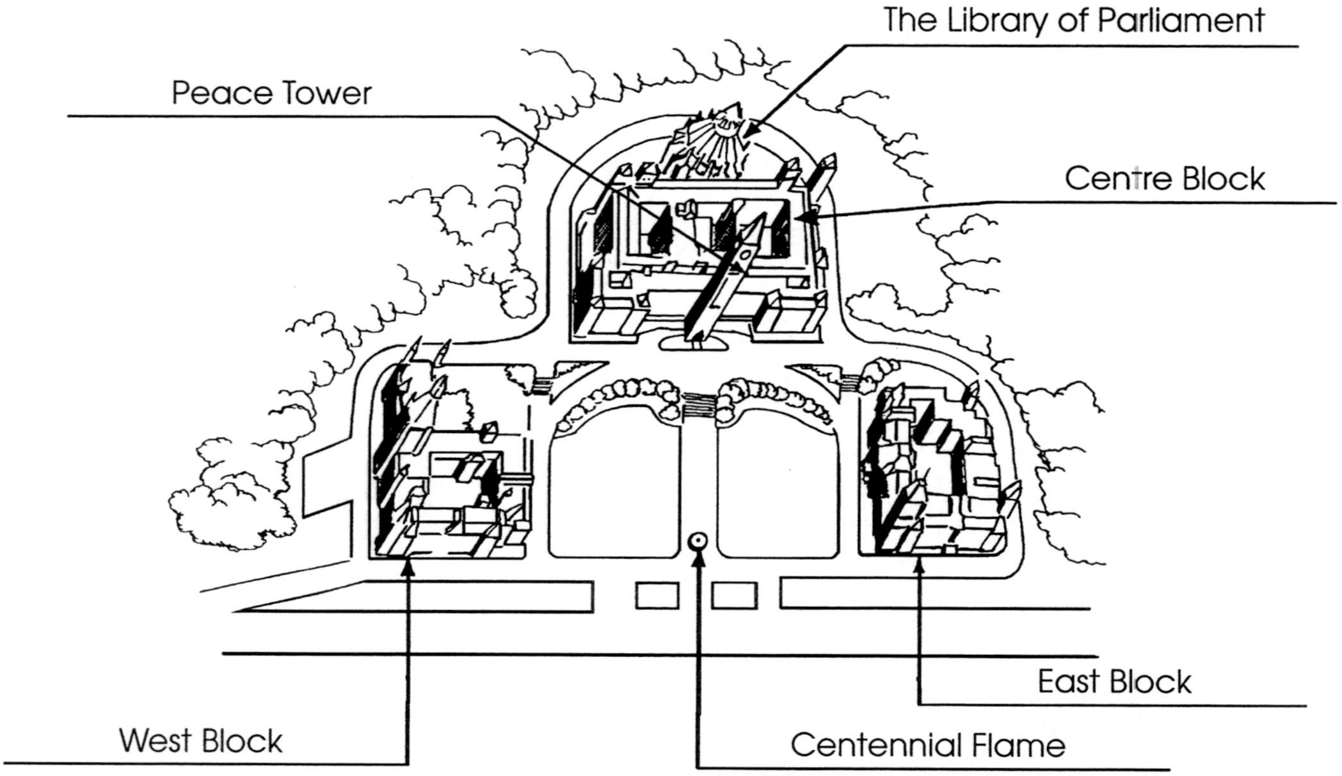

Parliament Hill is considered the heart of Canada's democratic system. The shape of the buildings on the hill has come to symbolize many of the values Canadians hold dear such as democracy, freedom of speech, tolerance, good citizenship and the sheer determination to thrive.

It is a meeting place where all Canadians can express themselves freely; a place where Canada's past, present and future come together; a centre of activity in every season.

Parliament Hill overlooks the **Ottawa River**, which marks the border between Ontario and Québec. This waterway was one of Canada's natural highways and today is used by touring boats and recreational crafts.

There are three important buildings on Parliament Hill. They are the Centre Block, the East Block and the West Block. The East and West Blocks were erected in the 1860's and are examples of High Victorian Gothic architecture. This style is characterized by multiple arches, high leaded-glass windows, massive flying buttresses, gargoyles and grotesques that watch from everywhere.

The Centre Block, the second building to stand at this location, dates back to the early 1920's and represents a neo-gothic style known as Modern Gothic. The Centre Block houses the chambers of the House of Commons and the Senate. The activities held in the chambers may be viewed from the Visitors' Gallery.

The Peace Tower is part of the Centre Block. It was built from 1919 to 1927 and was dedicated to the more than 60 000 Canadian soldiers who gave their lives on the battlefields of Europe during the First World War. It stands ninety metres tall and houses a carillon of fifty-three bells, a Memorial Chamber and an observation deck.

The **Summer Pavilion** was rebuilt in 1995 with contributions made by the Canadian Police Association. It is a memorial to honour brave men and women who were killed while performing their duties as police and peace officers. It is a place to visit to remember Canadian heroes.

On the 'Hill', numerous statues have been erected to honour famous Canadians who have shaped the history of Canada. Here, one can be in touch with Canada's history.

The Centennial Flame is found at the entrance to Parliament Hill. It was lit on January 1, 1967, by Prime Minister Lester B. Pearson to launch Canada's one hundredth anniversary celebrations. The flame is surrounded by the shields of the Canadian provinces and territories, and joined by the water of the fountain. The Centennial Flame symbolizes Canada's unity from sea to sea.

Parliament Hill is a place where one can view the past and present. It is fun to explore the grounds and buildings, to view historical monuments, or to watch politicians debating in the House of Commons and the Senate. On the Hill, one may see the **Changing of the Guard** ceremony or witness demonstrations by citizens who want their views to be heard. Perhaps the Prime Minister may be seen strolling around the grounds!

Name: ____________________

Parliament Hill

Answer the following questions with complete sentences.

1. What values do the buildings on Parliament Hill represent?

____

____

____

2. What are the names of the three main buildings located on Parliament Hill?

____

____

____

3. What makes the East and West Blocks such impressive-looking buildings?

____

____

4. Using a dictionary, locate the meanings of the following terms used in Victorian Gothic architecture.

    a) arch - ______________________________________

    ____

    b) buttress - ___________________________________

    ____

    c) gargoyle -___________________________________

    ____

    d) grotesque - __________________________________

    ____

5. In which building are the House of Commons and the Senate found?

____

____

6. Why is the Peace Tower a memorial?

____

____

7. What is the name of the building that was rebuilt to honour police officers killed in the line of duty?

____

____

8. Why were statues erected on Parliament Hill?

____

____

9. What does the Centennial Flame represent?

____

____

10. Using your favourite internet search engine, run a search using the key words "Parliament Hill Canada". Try to locate other interesting facts. Record three new facts on the lines provided.

____

____

____

____

____

____

The Statues of Parliament Hill

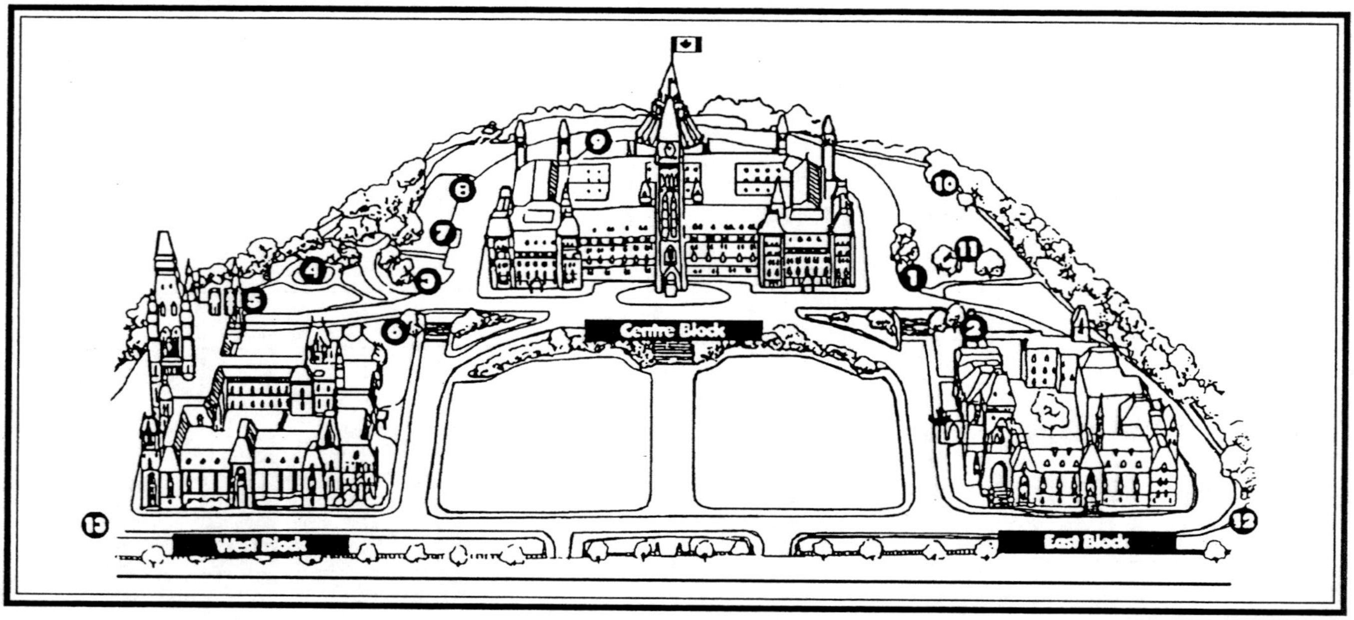

1. Sir John A. Macdonald
2. William Lyon Mackenzie King
3. Sir George-Étienne Cartier
4. Queen Victoria
5. Lester B. Pearson
6. John G. Diefenbaker
7. Alexander Mackenzie
8. George Brown
9. Thomas D'Arcy McGee
10. Robert Baldwin and Sir Louis-Hippolyte Lafontaine
11. Queen Elizabeth II
12. Sir Wilfred Laurier
13. Sir Robert Borden

A statue is an image of a person or animal carved in stone or wood, cast in metal, or moulded in clay or wax. Nearly every city in the world has a statue of some famous person who has contributed in some form to its growth and importance.

On Parliament Hill, there are numerous statues of famous people who have left their mark on Canada's history. There have been prime ministers, royalty and Fathers of Confederation who have been honoured.

1. **Sir John A. Macdonald's** statue represents his leadership as a Father of Confederation, his vision of a united country from ocean to ocean and his efforts to include all the provinces within the greater Canadian family. He became Canada's first Prime Minister after Confederation. His achievements have left an indelible mark on Canada's history.

2. **William Lyon Mackenzie King's** statue represents a dynamic and determined man who held power for almost twenty-two years (1921-1926, 1926-1930, 1935-1948). King introduced Canada's first social programs such as the Canada Pension Plan, unemployment insurance and family allowance. He also introduced Canadian citizenship.

3. **Sir George-Étienne Cartier** is remembered for his role as a Father of Confederation. This statue was unveiled in 1885 and was the first monument erected on Parliament Hill. The statues of Sir George-Étienne Cartier and Sir John A. MacDonald are perfectly symmetrical in relationship to the Centre Block. Sir John A. MacDonald stands on the right side of the building while Sir George-Étienne Cartier stands on the left side. This placement honours the remarkable and lasting friendship enjoyed by these two great political allies.

4. The statue of **Queen Victoria** was unveiled in 1901. After years of indecision, Queen Victoria chose the little lumber town as the capital of the Province of Canada. Her choice was an attempt to ease the political tensions of the day and to allow a new nation to emerge and grow. Her choice was a wise one as this lumber town now stands as one of the most beautiful capitals in the world.

5. **Lester B. Pearson** can be found sitting comfortably in an office chair. His statue is located close to Queen Victoria. He was Canada's fourteenth Prime Minister and did much to foster the image of Canada as a peaceful nation on the world stage.

6. **John G. Diefenbaker** was Prime Minister from 1957 to 1963. His legacy to Canada is the 'Canadian Bill of Rights' (1960).

7. **Alexander Mackenzie** was Prime Minister from 1873 to 1878. He gave Canadians the right to a secret ballot while voting.

8. **George Brown** helped form the 'Great Coalition' of the 1860's which brought about Confederation.

9. **Thomas D'Arcy McGee** was an important Father of Confederation. He was known for his powerful oratory and was a great advocate for a united Canada. He is often referred to as the first Canadian nationalist.

10. **Robert Baldwin** and **Sir Louis-Hippolyte Lafontaine** are seen standing together discussing an issue. They were the architects of the principle of responsible government adopted by the Province of Canada in 1848.

11. The statue of **Queen Elizabeth II** depicts her riding on her horse, Centennial, which was given to her by Canada. She has reigned over Canada since 1952.

12. **Sir Wilfred Laurier** made Ottawa a true capital city that all Canadians can look upon with pride. He was the first francophone Prime Minister of Canada from 1896 to 1911.

13. **Sir Robert Borden** led Canada during the First World War. In 1918, the Borden government introduced the 'Women's Franchise Act', giving women over eighteen who were British subjects the right to vote in federal elections.

Name: ____________________

Discover the Parliament Hill Statues

Read the information about the statues of Parliament Hill.

Record the number and name of the statue that each sentence is describing on the line provided.

1. He was Canada's fourteenth Prime Minister and his statue is located near a famous queen.

   ____

2. These men developed the principle of responsible government in 1848.

   ____

3. He was a dynamic and determined man who was Prime Minister for twenty-two years.

   ____

4. His statue stands on the right side of the Centre Block.

   ____

5. This Prime Minister worked hard to develop Canada's Bill of Rights.

   ____

6. She chose Ottawa as the capital of the Province of Canada.

   ____

7. This man was the first francophone Prime Minister of Canada.

   ____

8. He was an impressive speaker and fought hard as a Father of Confederation for a united Canada.

   ____

9. His monument was unveiled in 1885 and it was the first one to be erected on Parliament Hill.

   ____

10. The right to vote using a secret ballot was given during his term in office as Prime Minister.

    ____

11. This statue honours a famous queen and her horse.

    ____

12. This man was honoured for his work on the Great Coalition which brought about Confederation.

    ____

13. He led Canada during the First World War and gave women over eighteen the right to vote in federal elections.

    ____

14. His efforts and achievements left an indelible mark on Canada's history.

    ____

15. This Prime Minister and his government gave Canada the Canada Pension Plan, unemployment insurance and family allowance.

    ____

16. He had Ottawa changed from a drab ugly lumber town to a beautiful capital city of which Canadians are very proud.

    ____

17. She has been Queen over Canada for fifty years.

    ____

18. This Prime Minister introduced Canada's first social programs such as the Canada Pension Plan, unemployment insurance and family allowance.

    ____

Ottawa's Official Residences

Rideau Hall, 24 Sussex Drive, Stornoway, The Farm and 7 Rideau Gate are official residences located in and around Ottawa. These residences are provided by the Government of Canada for the Governor General, the Prime Minister, the Leader of the Opposition in the House of Commons, the Speaker of the House and official guests.

Rideau Hall is the official residence of the Governor General of Canada. It was built in 1838 in Bytown, now Ottawa, by Thomas Mackay, a Scottish stone mason, who had made his fortune as a contractor on the Rideau Canal and later as a mill owner. It was considered the finest home in Bytown.

The mansion was situated in the middle of a large estate. It contained five bedrooms, a library and several bathrooms with hot and cold running water. The home was surrounded by ornamental gardens, lawns, hedges and woods.

In 1866, the Mackay family rented the house to Governor General Monck, who moved to the new capital city from Québec City. In 1868, the government bought it for $82 000 from the Mackays. It then became the official residence of the Governor General of Canada and was the focal point of Ottawa's high society. Rideau Hall was known for its state dinners, skating parties and balls that would sometimes last until dawn. It provided a welcome escape from the muddy streets, noisy sawmills and harsh realities of living in a frontier capital.

Over the years, the addition of ballrooms, guest rooms, offices, a greenhouse, and curling rink now dwarf the original house. One interesting feature of the mansion is the 'Tent Room'; a wing that originally housed an indoor tennis court and is a favourite spot for state dinners. Kings, queens and presidents stay at Rideau Hall when they visit Canada's capital.

Rideau Hall is a national historic site and the symbolic home of all Canadians. It is open year-round (except during official functions) for visitors and the public to tour public rooms, the gardens and the greenhouse.

24 Sussex Drive

The official residence for Canada's Prime Minister is located at **24 Sussex Drive**. The house was built in 1866 by wealthy mill owner and Member of Parliament, Joseph Merrill Currier. In 1902, the house was sold to another lumber manufacturer, W.C. Edwards, who made many alterations to the house.

In 1943, the stone house was acquired by the federal government to be used as the official residence of the Prime Minister. The house was redesigned to give it a more formal appearance. It is magnificently situated on the cliffs above the Ottawa River, in sight of the Parliament Buildings. The first Prime Minister to live there was the Right Honourable Louis St. Laurent. Since then, all Prime Ministers have lived at 24 Sussex Drive during their term in office.

Stornoway

Stornoway is the official residence for the Leader of the Opposition. It is located at 541 Acacia Avenue in the village of Rockcliffe Park, near Ottawa. The house was built in 1914 for Asconio Major, an Ottawa grocer. The name 'Stornaway' was given to the house by its second owners, the Perley Robertsons, after their home in the Outer Hebrides in Scotland. It is a spacious two-storey home located on spacious grounds. During World War Two, Stornoway was a refuge for Crown Princess Juliana of the Netherlands and her daughters.

In 1950, concerned citizens raised money to make it the residence of the Official Leader of the Opposition. For twenty years, the house was maintained by donations. In 1970, the Canadian government acquired it for one dollar.

Mackenzie King Estate

The Mackenzie King Estate was bequeathed to the Canadian people by William Lyon Mackenzie King upon his death in 1950. On this estate are five country homes, barns, garages, gardens, walking trails, and the Moorside Ruins, a collection of materials from old Ottawa Buildings. One of the buildings, a 19th century farmhouse that King had restored, became an elegant year-round residence known as **The Farm**. This home is the official residence of the Speaker of the House of Commons.

Canada's official guest house provides a home for foreign dignitaries visiting Ottawa. It is called **7 Rideau Gate** and is located across the street from the residences of the Governor General and the Prime Minister. The house was built in 1862 for Henry Osgood Burrit. It was purchased by the federal government in 1966 as an official guest house.

7 Rideau Gate

Name: ____________________

Can You Name Ottawa's Official Residences?

Read the Information about Ottawa's official residences.

Complete each sentence with the name of the official residence it is describing.

Rideau Hall	**24 Sussex Drive**	**The Farm**
Stornoway	**7 Rideau Gate**	

1. ____________________ is located at 541 Acacia Avenue in the village of Rockcliffe Park, near Ottawa.

2. Canada's Prime Minister lives in a mansion called ____________________ which is its address.

3. The Speaker of the House lives in an elegantly restored 19th century farmhouse referred to as ____________________.

4. ____________________ is a national historic site which is open to the public all year.

5. During the Second World War, ____________________ provided a refuge for the royal family of the Netherlands.

6. ____________________ is part of the Mackenzie King Estate but is closed to the public.

7. Foreign dignitaries often stay at ____________________ while they are visiting Ottawa.

8. ____________________ was the main attraction for Ottawa's high society when it became the official residence for the Governor General in 1868.

9. A good view of the Ottawa River and the Parliament Buildings may be seen from ____________________.

10. ____________________ is located across the street from Rideau Hall and 24 Sussex Drive.

11. The official residence for the Speaker of the House is called ____________________.

12. The Canadian government purchased ____________________ for one dollar.

13. Kings, queens and presidents are often guests of the Governor General and stay at ____________________.

14. The first Prime Minister to live at ____________________ was the Right Honourable Louis St. Laurent.

15. ____________________ was built and owned by Thomas Mackay and it was said to be the finest home in Bytown.

16. Which official residence would you like to visit? Write a paragraph stating the reasons for your choice. Record the paragraph on the lines provided.

____

____

____

____

____

____

____

____

____

National Monuments of Canada

National War Memorial

The **National War Memorial** is located in Confederation Square in the heart of downtown Ottawa. It is a tribute to all Canadians who have served Canada in war. The monument represents dignity, pride, courage, friendship, and devotion to duty.

The Memorial stands 21 metres high and is made of a granite archway. Two bronze figures representing peace and freedom stand on top of the archway. In the centre of the monument is a large group of soldiers holding various fighting positions. They represent the 'Great Response' of thousands of Canadians who answered the call to serve during the First World War.

The Memorial was unveiled by his majesty King George VI in May 1939. It was designed by Vernon March of England, whose design was chosen in a world-wide competition in 1925.

Every November 11th, a solemn ceremony takes place at the National War Memorial. The Remembrance Day Ceremony is held here and it is televised across the country for all Canadians to watch.

The **Tomb of the Unknown Soldier** lies in front of the National War Memorial. On Sunday May 28, 2000, an important ceremony was held while the Unknown Soldier was buried in a special tomb.

The Tomb of the Unknown Soldier

The Tomb consists of a granite and bronze sarcophagus and contains the remains of an unidentified Canadian soldier from a cemetery near Vimy Ridge in France, the location of a famous Canadian victory during the First World War.

The Unknown Soldier represents the more than 116 000 Canadian men and women who have died in the service of their country. The **Tomb of the Unknown Soldier** is now the focal point for ceremonies that take place at the National War Memorial.

The **Reconciliation, Peacekeeping Monument** is the only one of its kind in the world. It is dedicated to Canadian peacekeepers.

Three bronze figures representing members of Canada's Armed Forces stand on top of high, converging walls that rise above the destruction of war. They are there to oversee and help mend differences. Canadian soldiers in previous wars fought battles to protect their country. Today Canada's Armed Services work in war-torn areas helping the people to restore order and to maintain peace in their country. The monument is located on Sussex Drive at the corner of St. Patrick Street in Ottawa.

The Reconciliation, Peacekeeping Monument

National Monuments of Canada

Research a Monument

There are many more monuments located in various cities and towns across Canada that have not been described in this book.

Using your favourite internet search engine, run a search using the key words "Canadian Memorial Monuments".

Click on the web site called 'We Will Remember War Monuments in Canada'.

Locate the name of your province or territory. Click on your province's or territory's name.

Click on the name of a monument.

View the monument's picture and read the information.

You may wish to view other monuments as well.

Choose the monument that was the most attractive and had an interesting description.

Write a brief report about it in on the worksheet provided.

Illustrate the monument.

Make sure your report answers all the journalistic questions:

Who? What? Why? When? Where? How?

Name of Monument

Canada's National Museums

Across our broad nation, there are many museums of various sizes that display Canadian heritage, different cultures, Canada's wildlife, forms of transportation and artifacts of the world. Did you know that Canada's capital city, Ottawa, has the highest concentration of museums in Canada? The museums appeal to a wide spectrum of interests such as science, history, art and aviation to name a few.

The **Canada Agricultural Museum** is a unique combination of a modern working farm and a museum. It is located on a two-hectare site on Ottawa's Experimental Farm, a 43-hectare farm that has been designated as a Heritage Site. The museum contains several heritage buildings, including the Dairy Barn, the Small Animal Barn and the Old Barn. As well as being a museum, the site is also a working farm. A wide variety of farm animals are seen on the premises such as a working dairy herd, sheep, pigs, goats, chickens, geese, rabbits, horses and a donkey. Special programs and exhibitions such as breadmaking, milking cows, butter making, ice cream making, and caring for cows entertain and educate visitors. What a wonderful place to become acquainted with farming in the past and present!

The **Canadian Museum of Civilization** is located on Laurier Street in Ottawa. The museum was designed and built to resemble a moving glacier, reminding people of the powerful forces that shaped our country.

The museum celebrates the diversity of people and displays the achievements of cultures past and present.

The Museum of Civilization is the largest museum. Inside Canada Hall you will find a West Coast native village complete with war canoes and totem poles. You may also walk through 1000 years of Canadian settlement beginning at the site of the earliest Viking Landing, through New France and Upper Canada, to the Prairies beyond. It is considered Ottawa's most popular attraction.

The **Canadian Postal Museum** displays artifacts that have played an important role in the Postal Service of Canada's past. The displays show how the mail has linked Canadians to each other and to the world. Familiar postal objects such as rural mailboxes, mailbags, mail carrier uniforms and the first Canadian stamp issued in 1851 may be viewed.

The **Canadian Museum of Nature** houses the many natural wonders found in our country. Canada's natural heritage may be seen in displays, exhibits and dioramas. The country's best mineral collection is one of the displays to be viewed. The birds and mammals of Canada may be observed in life-like dioramas.

The **Canadian War Museum** is an old castle-like structure that houses the military history of Canada. Our military history may be seen through life-size dioramas, displays and a magnificent display of war art. Live demonstrations are performed by costumed re-enactors. Musket demonstrations, concerts, and other special events take place in the courtyard.

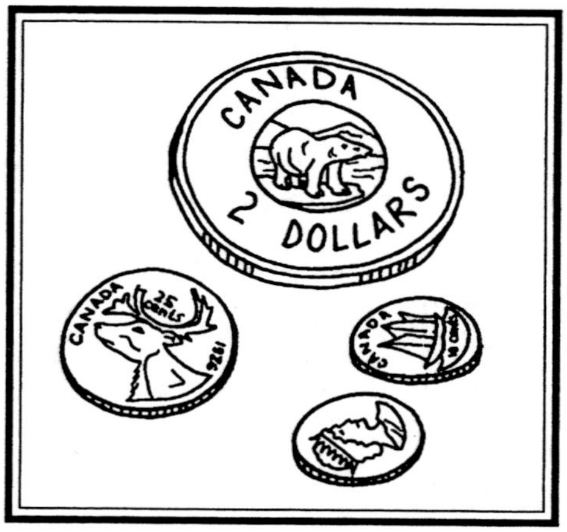

The **Currency Museum** of the Bank of Canada presents the most important collection of Canadian notes, coins and tokens in the world as well as currency from other countries. On display are a wide variety of artifacts used for exchange such as a stone weighing three tons, shells, glass beads, cocoa beans, tea and salt blocks, pelts, shark's teeth, merchant's tokens, playing-card money, and three and four dollar bank notes. The Currency Museum shows us the important role currency has upon the lives of Canadians and others around the world.

National Archives of Canada

The **National Archives of Canada** holds millions of different documents that pertain to Canada and Canadian history. The documents may be in the form of films, maps, diaries, treaties, art, government records, photographs, sound recordings and many more. Some of the artifacts are of unique value, and/or exceptionally beautiful while others are centuries old. They all reveal how we have lived in this place called Canada.

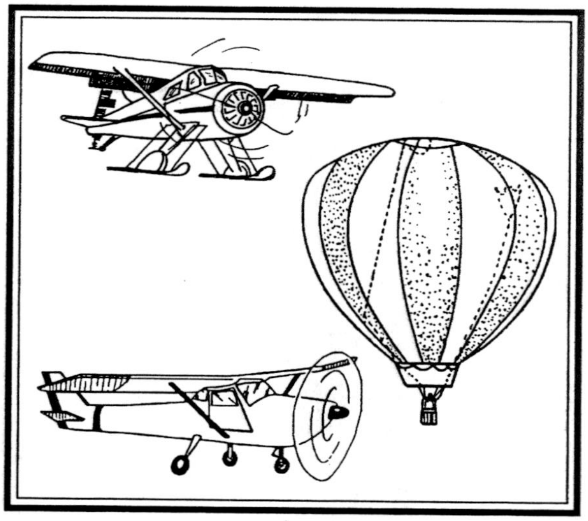

The **Canadian Aviation Museum** contains the finest collection of aeronautical machines in Canada. The aircraft illustrate the full story of air travel from the first attempts at flight to the jet age. On display is a Beaver and a Twin Otter which are bush planes used to open up rugged areas in Canada. They are one of Canada's most important contributions to international aviation. These types of planes and their designs are being used in rugged environments world wide. Old planes such as the Silver Dart and the Sopwith Snipe, used by World War Ace Billy Barker, may be viewed.

The **Canada Science and Technology Museum** focuses on Canadian accomplishments and their effect on the country. At this museum, one can view Canadian inventions from the snowmobile and electric stove to the Canadarm which is part of the space shuttle. This museum provides a hands-on experience for visitors as there are buttons to push, levers to pull, and dials to turn. Exhibits feature marine and land transportation, astronomy, communications, space, home, and computer technology. This museum had the largest retracting telescope in Canada for stargazers.

The **Laurier House National Historic Site** is a museum used to display the memorabilia of the political lives of two prominent Canadian Prime Ministers: Sir Wilfrid Laurier and William Lyon Mackenzie King. The home is located in a quiet residential neighbourhood close to Parliament Hill. Several rooms contain the mementos and furnishings of Sir Wilfrid Laurier. The majority of the house is restored to the King era and is filled with his collections of memorabilia and gifts from countries around the world.

The Laurier House

Name: ____________________

Where Would You Find It?

If you went to Ottawa for a visit, in which museum might you find the following items or activities?

Part A:

Record the number that is beside the name of the museum, on the line provided.

1. **The Canadian Agricultural Museum**
2. **The Canadian Museum of Civilization**
3. **The Canadian Postal Museum**
4. **The Canadian Museum of Nature**
5. **The Canadian War Museum**
6. **The Currency Museum of the Bank of Canada**
7. **The National Archives**
8. **The Canadian Aviation Museum**
9. **The Canada Science and Technology Museum**
10. **The Laurier House National Historic Site**

1. a collection of old Canadian stamps _____
2. muskets and canons used by early Canadian soldiers _____
3. plows, wagons and carriages used by the early settler farmers _____
4. a Canadian one and two dollar bill _____
5. a diorama of Canadian birds _____
6. photos of old Canadian buildings _____
7. the type of plane used by World War One pilots _____
8. displays of Canadian inventions _____
9. articles used for bartering in early Canada _____
10. cows being milked and sheep being sheared _____

11. an exhibit showing how mail was sorted by hand _____
12. exhibits showing military vehicles and military uniforms _____
13. watch a video showing the operations of a bank _____
14. a picture of a famous hockey player _____
15. an example of the early bush plane used to open up Canada's rugged north _____
16. see beautiful antique cars and giant steam locomotives _____
17. the crystal ball used by William Lyon Mackenzie King to seek the help of spirits in decision-making _____
18. a demonstration showing visitors how to make bread _____
19. a diary written by a former Prime Minister _____
20. the largest telescope in Canada _____

Part B:

People across our vast country are always trying to preserve our heritage and culture in a variety of museums.

Using your favourite internet search engine, run a search on the internet using the key words "Canada's Museums."

Look for the following types of museums and on the line provided record the name of the museum.

1. a cultural museum ________________________________
2. a sports museum ________________________________
3. a clothing museum ________________________________
4. a transportation museum________________________________
5. a food museum ________________________________
6. an insect museum ________________________________
7. a military museum ________________________________
8. a pioneer museum________________________________
9. a firefighter museum ________________________________

Canada's National Forts

Fort Henry

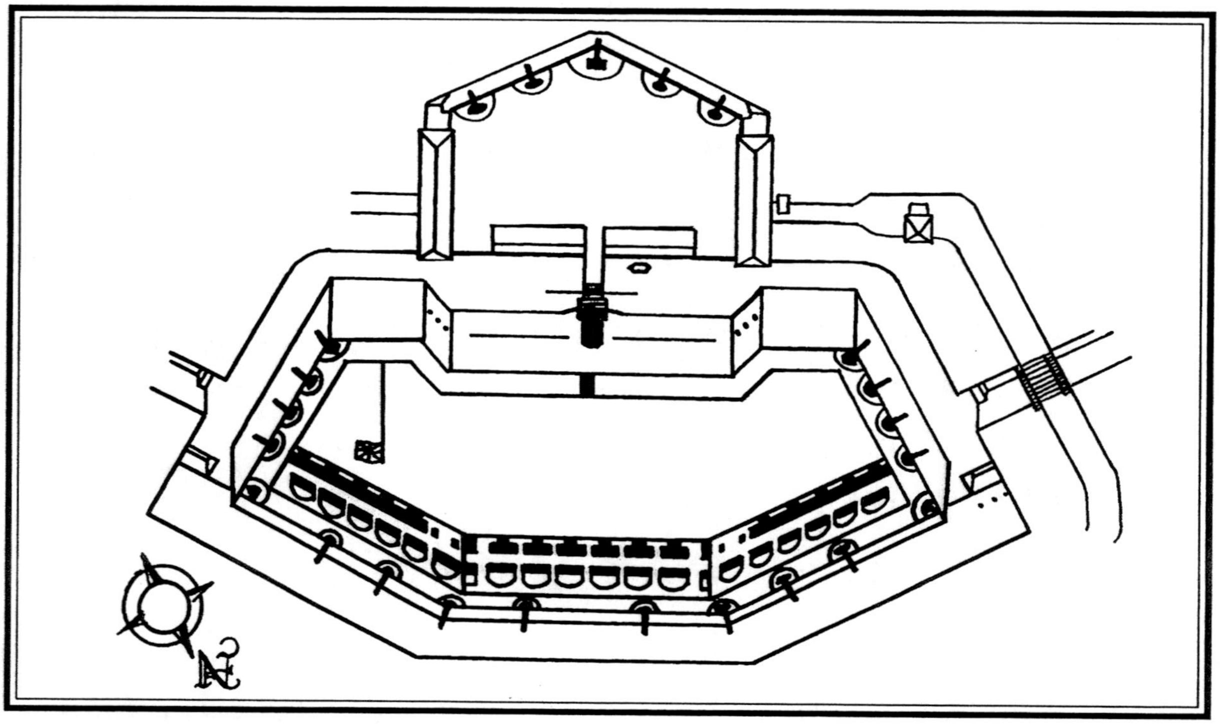

Fort Henry is a museum and a spectacular historic site located in Kingston, Ontario. The original Fort was built during the War of 1812 by Great Britain and the United States. It did not resemble the present fort in any way. Between 1832 and 1837, a second fort was built on the site of the first one, and it is this fort that stands there today. The Fort is located at Point Henry which is the intersection of three important waterways: the Rideau Canal System, the St. Lawrence River and Lake Ontario. The Fort was rebuilt to defend the area and its trading routes. Fort Henry was the largest fortification west of Québec City and cost 70 000 British pounds sterling to construct ($35 000 000 in modern Canadian currency).

In 1870, Fort Henry was abandoned by the British Army and was garrisoned by Canadian troops until 1891. It was then that Fort Henry began to show signs of disrepair. During World War One, the Fort was repaired and used as a prison for political prisoners. Following the war, the Fort fell into complete disrepair until 1936. During the next two years, the Fort was restored with money given by the federal and provincial governments. In August of 1938, the Fort was reopened as a museum and historic site as a "memorial to all British soldiers who served there" by Prime Minister William Lyon Mackenzie King.

During World War Two, Fort Henry became Camp 31, a Prisoner of War camp for enemy merchant seamen, soldiers, sailors, and airmen. In 1948, it was re-opened and is now a popular, well known tourist attraction.

Once inside the wooden gates, visitors discover the excitement and activities of 19th century military life. Guards perform drills and battle tactics. Fife and drum music accompanies the Garrison Parade. Lessons are taught at the Victorian School Room. David VII, Fort Henrys' Guards' goat mascot, may be met on his daily walkabouts and seen in the shows and parades put on by the Fort Henry Guards. Guided tours provide tourists with a view of many exhibits, museum rooms, and hidden passages.

One spectacular event is the Sunset Ceremonies. Visitors are entertained by bayonet drills and re-created battle tactics used over a century ago. Military music is played, guns fire thundering salutes, and fireworks light up the summer nights.

The Fortress of Louisbourg

The Fortress of Louisbourg was once one of the busiest harbours in North America and one of France's key centres of trade and military strength in the New World. In 1713, the French settled in Louisbourg on Isle Royale (Cape Breton Island) to continue fishing cod off the Grand Banks. In 1719, they began to build a fortified town. The town and settlement along the harbour shore soon became a thriving community. The cod fishery made

Isle Royale very prosperous. The fish was dried, salted and laid on racks which lined the streets of Louisbourg and its outports. The town was a hub of trading and commerce.

In 1745, during the war between Britain and France, the fortress was invaded and captured by the British from New England. In 1748, the town was given back to the French. In 1758, the British attacked the fortress a second time and captured it in seven weeks. This time, the British demolished its walls so that Louisbourg would never become a fortified French base.

In 1930, a museum was built and ruins and streets were uncovered on the site. In 1961, the Canadian government began a twenty-five million dollar project to reconstruct approximately one quarter of the original town and fortifications. The buildings, yards, gardens, and streets have been recreated as they were during the 1740's. This archaeological excavation has produced millions of artifacts as well as the ruins of fortification and buildings.

Each summer, the fortress comes alive and steps back in time to 1744. The streets of Rue Toulouse and Rue Royale are lined with period homes, exhibits, and theme centres. Costumed interpreters play the roles of the town's residents. Men, women, and children perform activities that would be done by the rich and poor during that time period. The residents entertain visitors with their stories, dances, music, nailmaking, cooking, sewing, gardening, and much more.

Delicious food and beverages, based on 18th century traditions and recipes, are prepared and served in the three period restaurants. It is indeed an experience to eat, using only a large spoon, where townspeople and off-duty soldiers eat, drink, gamble, and chat.

Activity

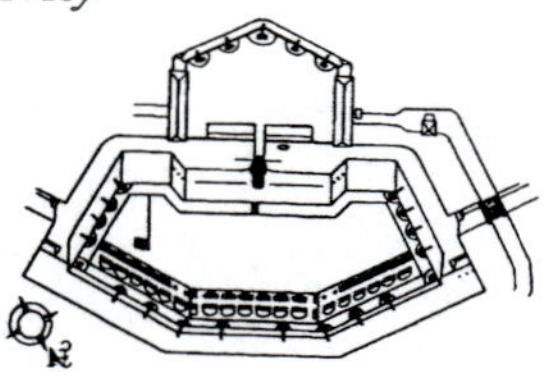

Name: ____________________

Canada's National Forts

When Did It Happen?

Read the information entitled Canada's National Forts.

Locate the date or time when each of the events took place. Record the date or time on the line provided at the end of each event.

1. Fort Henry was abandoned by the British Army. __________
2. The French settled in Louisbourg on Isle Royale. __________
3. Fort Henry was re-opened as a historical tourist attraction. __________
4. The first Fort Henry was built by Britain and the United States. ________________________________
5. A museum was built on the site where Louisbourg once stood. __________
6. The French settlers began to build Louisbourg, a fortified town. __________
7. The second Fort Henry was built on the site of the original one. ________________________________
8. Fort Henry was repaired and used as a prison for political prisoners. ________________________________
9. Archaeological excavation and restoration work was started on Louisbourg. __________
10. The British captured Louisbourg a second time and destroyed its walls. __________
11. Fort Henry was restored and opened as a museum and historic site by Prime Minister Mackenzie King. ____________________
12. Fort Henry was used as Camp 31, a Prisoner of War Camp. ________________________

Activity

Name: ____________________

Canada's National Forts

Let's Use the Internet!

Canada's early settlements were fortified communities built by the British and the French military, fur traders, and settlers. They are found in nearly every province and territory.

Using your favourite internet search engine run a search on the internet using the key words "Forts of Canada" to locate the names of forts located in Canada.

Read the list of web sites to find the key words 'Canadian Forts' and then click on them.

At this website, locate the name of your province or territory. Click on its name.

Record the names of five forts, their location in the province or territory, and one interesting fact about each one.

Use the following chart to record your information.

Fort	Location	Interesting fact

Canadian Castles

No one would ever imagine that castles could be found in Canada. In Europe, castles were built by kings and queens to house their royal families, store their treasures and to protect their lands. In Canada, castles were built by very wealthy men who wanted to show off their wealth.

One famous castle called **Casa Loma** is located in Toronto, Ontario. Casa Loma, which means "house on the hill", was the dream of Toronto businessman Sir Henry Pellatt. He wanted to create a 'medieval' castle on the brow of a hill overlooking the City of Toronto.

Casa Loma

In 1911, the work on the castle began and it took three hundred men to build it costing $3 500 000 at that time. Sir Henry enjoyed living in Casa Loma for less than ten years and had to abandon his cherished home because of financial misfortune. The castle is now owned by the City of Toronto and is a popular tourist attraction.

Toronto's famous castle consists of decorated rooms, secret passageways, a 240 metre tunnel, towers, stables, and two hectares of beautiful gardens.

Dundurn Castle

Dundurn Castle is located in Hamilton, Ontario. Sir Allan Napier MacNab had it built for his wife and family. Construction began in 1832 and the castle was completed in 1835.

Dundurn Castle had seventy-two rooms which were lavishly decorated with oak panelling and huge chandeliers. It was equipped with the newest technology such as running water and gas lighting.

Lavish parties and meetings were held at Dundurn Castle which attracted important people from Canada and Britain. After MacNab's death in 1862, the castle was sold to pay for the enormous debts he had accumulated.

Down through the years, Dundurn Castle has passed through the hands of several owners. It was left deserted and neglected. Donald MacInnes, the last owner, convinced the City of Hamilton to buy it in 1899. Since then the grounds have been made open to the public and the castle has been restored and made into a museum.

Craigdarroch Castle

Craigdarroch Castle is located on the highest spot in Victoria, British Columbia. It was built for Robert Dunsmuir between 1887 and 1890 with the finest materials from across the North American continent. The castle cost approximately $500 000. It was a landmark and a monument to his wealth.

Robert Dunsmuir passed away before the castle was finished in 1889. Mrs. Dunsmuir and her children moved into the castle in 1890. After her death in 1908, the Dunsmuir daughters had the estate subdivided into 144 residential lots. One large parcel of land was reserved for the castle and its grounds. The castle was then raffled off as a prize to the people who bought the residential lots. The winner later lost Craigdarroch to the Bank of Montreal in 1919.

Eventually the City of Victoria purchased the property. It has been used for a military hospital, the home of Victoria College, offices for the Victoria School Board, the Conservatory of Music and finally as a heritage house museum under the care of a historical museum society.

Activity

Name: ____________________

Canada's Castles

Name That Castle!

Read the information entitled Canada's Castles.

Locate the name of the castle that each sentence is describing. Record the castle's name on the line provided in each sentence.

1. ____________________ was built for Robert Dunsmuir and his family and cost approximately five hundred thousand dollars.
2. ____________________ was equipped with running water and gas lighting.
3. ____________________ was the dream home of business man, Henry Pellatt.
4. ____________________ was built for Sir Allan Napier MacNab in Hamilton, Ontario.
5. It took three hundred men and over three million dollars to build ____________________.
6. Robert Dunsmuir's daughters held a raffle for ____________________ after their mother's death.
7. ____________________ was eventually left empty and neglected by its owners.
8. ____________________ had rooms that were panelled with wood and lit by huge chandeliers.
9. Robert Dunsmuir died before ____________________ was completed in 1889.
10. Sir Henry Pellatt had to leave ____________________ because he could no longer afford to keep it.
11. ____________________ was built on the highest spot in Victoria because Robert Dunsmuir wanted everyone to know how wealthy he was.
12. Secret passages, a very long tunnel, beautiful rooms, and towers are found in ____________________.
13. ____________________ was used for a military hospital and a college before it became a historical museum.
14. ____________________ is a medieval castle sitting on the top of a hill overlooking the City of Toronto.
15. The lavish parties held at ____________________ attracted important people from Canada and Britain.

Canada's Historic Homes

In most towns and cities across our broad country one can find a historical home of a famous Canadian. At some time in Canada's past, this person has played an important role in the growth of the community, the province, or the country. Let's visit just a few of these homes.

Bellevue House

Bellevue House is located in Kingston, Ontario. It was at one time the home of Sir John A. Macdonald, Canada's first Prime Minister and his wife.

Bellevue House is one of the earliest and finest examples of Italian Villa architecture found in Canada. This impressive white stucco house, trimmed in green, with its red roof, proudly stands amidst flower gardens, pathways, orchards, and a kitchen garden. Sir John A. Macdonald hoped his wife's chronic ill-health would improve in this quiet, secluded atmosphere.

Parkwood Estate was once the home of R.S. McLaughlin, owner of General Motors of Canada. It is located on four hectares of land in the middle of Oshawa close to the hospital. Parkwood was his home from 1917 until his death at one hundred years of age.

Parkwood Estate

On the estate is a fifty-five room mansion, a large green house and a wide variety of gardens filled with beautiful flowers and shrubs. Visitors can tour over thirty of the rooms filled with priceless antiques and rugs from all over the world. Hand painted murals, rich tapestries and a gilded, hand-painted Steinway piano delight many a visitor.

In his will, R.S. Mc Laughlin bequeathed his estate to the Oshawa General Hospital, now called Lakeridge-Health Oshawa, to be used for its expansion. Today, it is used as a tourist attraction and has become a popular movie location for filming. This wonderful estate represents the luxurious lifestyle enjoyed by a rich, famous, and generous Canadian.

Green Gables

Green Gables is the home L. M. Montgomery used as the setting for her novel *Anne of Green Gables*. It located in Prince Edward Island National Park.

In real life, the farm was owned by David and Margaret MacNeil, who were cousins of L.M. Montgomery's grandfather. Although L.M. Montgomery never lived there, she grew up nearby with her grandparents. She explored the farm and surrounding woodlands and knew them well. She discovered places and named them such as 'Lover's Lane' and the 'Haunted Woods'.

The Green Gables site has been restored with the reconstruction of period farm outbuildings such as a barn, granary, and woodshed. The house has been restored to the period of the later 1800's as well as the setting in the novel.

Every summer, thousands of tourists from all over the world stroll through the humble green and white frame house and follow the trails through the shady forest while listening to the babbling brook of L. M. Montgomery's childhood.

Robert Service Cabin

In Dawson City, Yukon sits a little log cabin on Eighth Avenue. This was once the home to the world's most famous Yukoner, Robert Service. The two-room log cabin sits among willows and alders on a hillside overlooking the city.

Robert Service was born in England in 1874. In 1896, he came to Canada and travelled to the Yukon to work as a bank clerk at the Bank of Commerce in Whitehorse, then Dawson City. While living in this log cabin, which he never owned, he was inspired to write some of his most famous poems and a book that became a Hollywood motion picture. Service was known as the 'Bard of the Yukon' who immortalized the Klondike Gold Rush in such classics as *The Shooting of Dan McGrew* and *The Cremation of Sam McGee*.

Emily Carr's Home

Emily Carr has become known as one of Canada's most famous artists. She was a painter and a writer who lived in Victoria, British Columbia. Her paintings reflected dark, imposing landscapes and native artifacts of the West Coast.

Emily Carr built and lived in a small apartment house, the **House of All Sorts**, for twenty-five years. The apartment house had two suites. Emily hoped the income from the house would provide her with money so she could paint full time. Unfortunately this did not happen as she became a landlady, cook, potter, gardener, breeder of dogs and part-time painter during her years at the House of All Sorts.

Today, tourists wander through the house to view the Doll's House, the Studio, Lower West Flat, and Lower East Flat. Some even climb up the attic ladder to see 'Emily's eagles' painted on the roof.

Louis Riel's Home

Louis Riel, a Métis, was born in Saint Boniface, Manitoba in 1844. He led several rebellions against the Canadian government fighting for the Métis right to own their own land and their political rights. The Canadian government exiled him and eventually found him guilty of treason and he was executed in Regina in November 1885.

Today the **Riel Home** may be viewed by tourists in South St. Vital, Manitoba on the banks of the Red River. The house is displayed in the same manner as it would be found in the spring of 1886. It is a house of mourning, displaying the family's grief after Riel's execution. The roof bears a black cross and in the parlour, black crepe is draped over a picture of Louis Riel.

The home also reflects many aspects of Métis and European culture. Items such as store-bought oil lamps and clocks accompany handmade rawhide-strung chairs and homespun cloth. An aboriginal hammock for a baby and a European-style cradle are present as well in the parlour. The cast iron stove was used to keep the twelve family members warm during winter months. The Riels had a large family and compared with other settlers were relatively well off.

Activity

Name: ____________________

Canada's Historic Homes

Where is it Located?

Part A:

Read the information entitled Canada's Historic Homes.

Find out the location of each home mentioned in the information story. Record each answer on the line provided.

1. Parkwood Estate ____________________
2. House of All Sorts ____________________
3. Robert Service Cabin ____________________
4. Green Gables ____________________
5. Bellevue House ____________________
6. Riel House ____________________

Part B:

Record the name of each historic home that answers each question on the line provided.

1. Which home was an impressive mansion? ____________________
2. Which home was built to look like an Italian villa? ____________________
3. Which house is a humble green and white frame home?

   ____
4. Which home was owned by a famous Canadian painter?

   ____
5. Which home was made of logs and had only two rooms?

   ____
6. Which home shows that a tragic event had taken place in the family?

   ____
7. In which home did a Prime Minister once live?

   ____
8. Which home was owned by a millionaire?

   ____
9. Which home became famous due to the writings of a famous author?

   ____
10. Which house contains artifacts of two different cultures?

    ____
11. Which home was left to a medical institution?

    ____

Famous Bridges of Canada

Due to the many large rivers found in Canada, communities located on each side of it are often linked with a structure called a bridge. Some are large steel structures, some are made of wood, some are covered, and some are able to raise or swing around to allow ships and boats to pass through.

The Hartland Covered Bridge

The **Hartland Covered Bridge** is located in a small New Brunswick community called Hartland. It is the longest covered bridge in the world measuring 390 metres in length. The bridge was built from cedar, spruce and hard pine. It spans the Saint John River, one of the largest rivers in Canada. Citizens from both sides of the river contributed money for its building and it was officially opened July 4, 1901.

In 1906, the New Brunswick government purchased the bridge. Two spans of the Bridge were taken out by river ice on April 6, 1921. The government made repairs and covered the structure in 1922. A side walkway was added in 1947 for pedestrians. On June 23, 1980, the Hartland Covered Bridge was declared a National Historic Site. Today, tourists from all over the world flock to see this famous covered bridge where sweethearts of days gone by stopped their horse and buggies to steal a kiss or two.

The **Peace Bridge** was built to connect Buffalo, New York with Fort Erie, Canada. The bridge is one of North America's most important ports. Four thousand trucks cross the Peace Bridge daily. Over one million commercial vehicles use it each year.

The Peace Bridge consists of five arched spans over the Niagara River and a Parker throughtruss which spans the Black Rock Canal on the American side. The total length of the bridge is 1770 metres. It consists of 1188 metres of steel work and includes seventy-two metric tons of reinforcing steel.

The Peace Bridge

The Peace Bridge was officially opened in 1927 to commemorate one hundred years of peace between the United States and Canada.

The Confederation Bridge

Confederation Bridge is the longest bridge built over ice covered waters in the world. It is 12.9 kilometres long and crosses the Northumberland Strait at its narrowest point connecting Borden-Carleton, Prince Edward Island and Jourimain, New Brunswick. Confederation Bridge is eleven metres wide from guardrail to guard-rail including one lane and one emergency shoulder in each direction.

The bridge was built of reinforced concrete and consists of forty-four spans that are forty metres off the water. It has three hundred and ten street lights to light it and seventeen closed circuit television cameras providing surveillance coverage. Emergency telephones and fire extinguishers are provided every 750 metres. The 1.1 metre high concrete barriers on the bridge prevent drivers from seeing directly down over the side of it as well as acting as a windbreak. The bridge is curved to prevent drivers from becoming distracted. Message signs located at the end of the bridge inform drivers about driving conditions on it.

The opening of Confederation Bridge on May 31, 1997, brought a new age of transportation to Atlantic Canada. The bridge carries two lanes of traffic twenty-four hours a day, seven days a week. It takes approximately ten minutes to cross it at a normal speed.

The **Lion's Gate Bridge** spans the First Narrows of Burrard Inlet in the city of Vancouver, British Columbia. The bridge was named after the twin snow-capped peaks that stand like guardians over the harbour below. The peaks are known as the Lions and were the inspiration for the name of the new bridge. A sculptor was hired to create a monument to both the

The Lion's Gate Bridge

bridge and the peaks. On either side of the Lion's Gate Bridge's south entrance stand large stone lions. On May 19, 1939, King George VI and Queen Elizabeth, his wife, attended the official opening.

The Lion's Gate Bridge is one of the oldest and best used of the fifteen bridges in Vancouver. The three-lane bridge carries twenty-five million vehicle trips per year. The Lion's Gate Bridge spans the entrance to Vancouver Harbour, Canada's gateway to the Pacific Rim.

The **Capilano Suspension Bridge** is located in Vancouver, British Columbia as well. The thirty-five metre suspension bridge is stretched across a canyon sixty-nine metres above Vancouver's spectacular Capilano River. Although it often sways and creaks in the wind, it is able to support the weight of ten heavy duty military fighter planes. More than 850 000 visitors cross it each year.

The Capilano Suspension Bridge

The original Capilano Suspension Bridge was built by George MacKay in the late 1800's. With the help of local natives and a team of horses, he suspended a hemp rope and cedar plank bridge across the river. Natives called it the 'laughing bridge' because of the noise it made when the wind blew through the canyon. George MacKay had a dream to develop the area as a recreational wonderland but died before he could see it actually take place.

In 1903, the hemp rope bridge was replaced by a wire cable bridge. In 1910, Edward Mahon bought the property and developed the town of North Vancouver and established the Capilano Suspension Bridge as a major recreational attraction. Since then various owners have improved the site making it a popular tourist attraction.

Today, visitors can view the colourful totem poles that are on display and watch First Nation Carvers work while they tell their ancient stories. They can take a walk on the suspension bridge to the other side of the canyon to view the flora and fauna of the West Coast rainforest.

Activity 

Name: ____________________

Famous Canadian Bridges

Read the information on Famous Bridges in Canada.

Record the word **True** or **False** on the line at the end of each statement.

1. The Hartland Covered Bridge is the longest bridge in the world. __________
2. The Peace Bridge was built to celebrate one hundred years of peace between Canada and the United States. __________
3. The Lion's Gate Bridge spans the Northumberland Strait connecting New Brunswick and Prince Edward Island. __________
4. The first Capilano Suspension Bridge was made of hemp rope and cedar planks. __________
5. At the south entrance of the Peace Bridge stand two large stone lions on each side. __________
6. The Hartland Covered Bridge spans the Saint John River in New Brunswick. __________
7. On the Peace Bridge there are emergency phones and fire extinguishers every 750 metres. __________
8. The Capilano Suspension Bridge spans the entrance to Vancouver Harbour in British Columbia.
9. The Hartland Covered Bridge was severely damaged by river ice in 1921. __________
10. The Lion's Gate Bridge was named after twin snow-capped mountain peaks. __________
11. The Peace Bridge is 12.9 kilometres wide and spans the Niagara River and the Black Rock Canal. __________
12. Confederation Bridge was built of reinforced concrete and has forty-five spans measuring forty metres off the water. __________
13. The Hartland Covered Bridge and the Capilano Suspension Bridge are popular tourist attractions in Canada. __________
14. The Lion's Gate Bridge was once called the 'laughing bridge' by local natives. __________
15. The Peace Bridge is one of North America's most important ports that connects Buffalo, New York with Fort Erie, Canada. __________

Canada's Famous Towers

A tower is a structure whose height is much greater than its width. It is usually taller than any other structures surrounding it. A tower may stand alone or be part of a wall or a building. Early towers were built for military defence or religious purposes. Today, towers are used for communication and tourist attractions.

The Martello Tower

Martello Towers were built in British North America between 1796 and 1846. Sixteen squat, flat-roofed towers were built in strategic places to ward off invading attackers in the following sites: Halifax (5), Saint John (1), Québec City (4), Kingston (6).

The Martello Towers located in Kingston were built in 1846-1848 due to the border tensions with the United States; they were designed the best. A Martello Tower was entered by a doorway in the second storey or barracks floor. The ground floor contained storage space and a powder magazine. The tower's flat roof was meant to accomodate artillery pieces and was surrounded by a parapet. The thick walls were constructed of stone which was able to absorb artillery fire.

None of the Martello Towers were ever attacked. Eleven have survived the ravages of time and some are used as museums and tourist attractions.

The **Peace Tower** on Parliament Hill in Ottawa is recognized by people all over Canada. It is a free-standing bell tower located in front of the Centre Block of Canada's Parliament Buildings. Its walls are made of Nepean sandstone that rise 92.2 metres from the base to the bronze flagpole. The tower's roof is made of reinforced concrete covered with copper.

The Peace Tower

The Peace Tower contains an observation deck, a clock with four faces, a carillon of bells and the Memorial Chamber. The Memorial Chamber is dedicated to the Canadian men and women who gave their lives in the service of their country during wartime. The Books of Remembrance , in which the names of Canadians who died in battle have been written, are found here.

The Skylon Tower

The **Skylon Tower** is located in Niagara Falls, Ontario. It was built during the years 1964 - 1965 as a tourist attraction. The Skylon Tower soars 236 metres above the Niagara Gorge and overlooks both the Canadian and American Falls. Breath-taking views can be seen of the area from the observation deck of the Tower.

The 'slip-form' technique of building was used to construct the tower. Concrete was poured continuously around the clock for thirty-eight days. The 'slip-form', which measured one metre, was moved upward slowly by hydraulic jacks. The tapered shape of the tower was achieved by reducing the size of the slip-form.

The 'Dome' was the most difficult part of the structure to assemble and place. The circular form for the base of the dome was 33.2 metres across and it was assembled on the ground level around the base of the tower. The form was raised 11.9 metres in the air to prepare for the pouring of cement. Once the cement had dried, the form was lowered to the ground.

Today the Skylon Tower's Dome houses a revolving dining room, an indoor/outdoor observation deck and gift shops. On a clear day, visitors can see close to 8000 square kilometres of Canada and the United States including the skylines of Toronto and Buffalo.

The **CN Tower** was built by the Canadian National Railways, or CN, as a transmission tower that would stand taller than any of the tallest Toronto buildings. It was built to improve signals delivered to televisions in Toronto homes.

Work on the foundation began in 1973 with giant backhoes excavating 56000 metric tons of earth and shale to a depth of fifteen metres.

The CN Tower

Prestressed concrete and reinforced steel were arranged in a Y-shaped pattern 6.6 metres thick. Each hollow leg of the Y would carry its fair share of the tower's 181.8 metric ton burden. The foundation took four months to complete.

The next section of the tower was made from a huge mould called a 'slip-form' that moved upward as the poured concrete hardened. The mould gradually decreased in width giving the tower its shape. At the 330 metre mark, the builders prepared to build the 'Sky Pod', a seven-storey structure housing two observation decks, a revolving restaurant, a nightclub and broadcasting equipment. The Sky Pod is reached by four high-speed, glass-fronted elevators whose rapid rise provides visitors with a very thrilling ride.

Above the Sky Pod is found the 'Space Deck', 488 metres up. Breathtaking views from the glass-enclosed balcony may be viewed by visitors. On a good day sites that are120 kilometres away may be seen.

The last phase of the tower was the one hundred metre communication mast. A Sikorsky Skycrane helicopter lifted forty six metric ton sections into place. The completed mast was then encased in a fibreglass reinforced sheath to prevent icing.

The CN Tower was completed in 1975 costing fifty-seven million dollars. It is the tallest free-standing structure in the world and proudly takes ownership of Toronto's skyline.

Name: ____________________

Canadian Towers Crossword Puzzle

Read the Information entitled Canada's Famous Towers.

Carefully read each puzzle clue. Complete the crossword puzzle by locating answers from the information.

Canadian Towers Crossword Puzzle

Puzzle Clues

Across

1. top part of the CN Tower
2. can be seen in Toronto
3. the number of elevators in the CN Tower
4. located in Niagara Falls
5. a special room in the Peace Tower
6. a building material used in the CN Tower and the Skylon Tower
7. location of the tower with the gorgeous view
8. a tall structure

Down

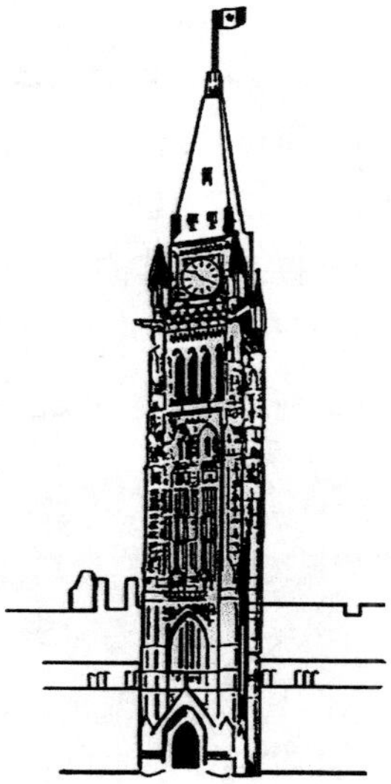

1. squat, flat-roofed towers used for defence
2. soldiers' names are listed in it
3. Peace Tower stands in front of this building
4. a method used to build free-standing towers
5. a seven-storey structure that's part of the CN Tower
6. a dining room that turns three hundred and sixty degrees
7. a free-standing bell tower
8. the number of Martello Towers built in Canada

Canadian Heritage Towns and Villages

A heritage town or village is usually created by people living in a community who want to preserve its historical development. A collection of buildings which are of significant historic interest and value are shown. The buildings are filled with articles that represent the period of time in which they were built. Throughout Canada there are many heritage towns and villages. Some are quite large and have become popular sites that attract tourists.

Upper Canada Village is located outside of Morrisburg, Ontario. It is a bustling mid-19th century community, found on the shores of the mighty St. Lawrence River, in which Canadian history comes alive.

The Village was created by moving historic buildings to one area. It was carefully reproduced as a complete 19th century community. The furnishings, fabrics, farm and industrial machinery were very carefully selected. The village has working farms, factories, mills, tradeshops, and finished homes.

There are many exciting events and activities taking place every day at the Village. Costumed interpreters demonstrate activities from the spinning of wool in a log house to the grinding of wheat into flour in a steam-powered mill. The Village may be toured in a horse-drawn wagon, an old fashioned train, or in a tow scow (a flat-bottomed boat).

Kings Landing Historical Settlement is located on the banks of the Saint John River in New Brunswick. It is a living museum that vibrantly brings to life the story of the early settlers who lived in the Saint John Valley from 1790 - 1910.

Visitors enjoy watching farmers caring for historic gardens and tending old-breed livestock. Antique farming equipment powered by horse and oxen may be met on the village roadways or seen in rail-fenced fields.

Costumed interpreters entertain visitors in the eleven historic homes with activities and tasks performed in early settler days such as spinning, weaving, sewing, baking bread, open hearth cooking, and candle-making. Tradesmen such as the cooper, blacksmith, carpenter, and miller demonstrate their skills. Delicious meals cooked using old recipes and early cooking methods may be enjoyed at the Kings Head Inn and the English-style pub.

Every day at Kings Landing is an exciting and informative window through which people may view a way of life experienced by the United Empire Loyalists.

In New Brunswick on the Rivière du-Nord near the town of Caraquet lies an **Acadian Historical Village**. The Village reflects the way of life that Acadians experienced during 1770 - 1890.

There are fifty buildings in the Village that are original and made from roughly hewn timbers. The homes are usually one large room with an attic or loft area used for storage. The large room was used by the entire family for working, eating and sleeping. The homes are furnished with only the necessities and display the life of poverty and hardship endured by very early French settlers.

The Acadian Historical Village is staffed with bilingual interpreters, dressed in period costumes, who bring customs and traditional trades back to life in original buildings. The Village has a cooper's shop, a lobster hatchery, a tinsmith shop, a covered bridge, and the Château Albert which is a hotel where tourists can spend the night. The interpreters spin, weave, hammer hot metals on a forge, and set type for a newspaper. Grain is grown on low land reclaimed from the sea by a dyking system developed by early French settlers.

Horse-drawn carts will take you past many sights displaying the Acadians' tale of their struggle to survive after their expulsion by the British.

Barkerville Historic Town is located in the Cariboo Mountains, eighty kilometres east of Quesnel in British Columbia. In 1862, Billy Barker found gold at Williams Creek and this discovery began the famous Cariboo Gold Rush. Thousands of people travelled the Cariboo Wagon Trail between 1862 and 1870 converging on the boom town. During the gold rush days, Barkerville was the largest town in the Canadian West.

Today, Barkerville lives on as a town of discovery with one hundred and twenty reconstructed buildings on display. Interpreters and a troupe of actors portray characters from Barkerville's past to give visitors a first hand experience of life in the Gold Rush era. Wild stories and lively songs enjoyed by miners over one hundred years ago can still be heard at the Theatre Royal. Famous Judge Begbee, a professional actor, retells the story of the struggle to bring British justice to the wild frontier in British Columbia in the Richfield Courthouse.

On the banks of Williams Creek, the massive Cornish Wheel is put into operation. Daniel Grimsby and Jack Beaman, early miners, demonstrate how the wheel works. Everyone loves to watch the town blacksmith at work making his anvil sing with the blows of his mighty hammer as he turns some iron into a tool or implement. The delicious smell of sourdough bread often entices visitors into the local bake shop for a taste. Foamy old-style root beer may be sipped in the saloon of the hotel. Travelling through town in a stagecoach shows the sights and sounds that early Gold Rush travellers experienced on their arrival.

Activity

Name: ____________________

Heritage Word Search

Read the information entitled Heritage Towns and Villages in Canada.

In the word search, **twenty** words are hidden that refer to the historic towns and villages written about in the information.

Circle the words in the puzzle and then record them on the lines provided.

C	A	R	I	B	O	O	W	A	G	O	N	T	R	A	I	L	Z	Y	R	H	E	R	I	T	A	G	E	F	C	S
A	S	R	N	A	Q	V	P	N	W	O	X	O	N	Y	M	Z	L	A	K	B	J	B	C	A	M	T	R	H	G	O
R	T	U	T	R	O	U	N	T	M	T	L	W	K	C	J	R	A	I	S	H	G	K	C	F	T	E	I	U	D	U
I	P	V	E	K	Q	B	R	I	S	H	I	S	T	O	R	I	C	E	A	R	Z	I	D	Y	X	C	W	D	V	R
B	X	U	R	E	S	R	Q	Q	P	T	O	C	N	S	M	L	A	F	K	E	G	N	H	E	I	F	J	G	H	D
O	V	Y	P	R	W	Z	A	U	P	B	O	O	C	T	D	N	D	E	M	V	F	G	G	T	H	L	I	K	J	O
O	Q	C	R	V	R	D	S	E	T	E	U	W	V	U	W	F	I	X	G	I	Y	S	H	R	Z	A	I	B	J	U
M	X	N	E	I	V	Y	U	Z	T	A	S	B	R	M	C	Q	A	D	P	R	O	L	N	A	M	E	L	F	K	G
O	G	H	T	L	I	M	U	S	E	U	M	J	F	E	K	E	N	L	D	E	M	A	N	D	O	P	G	Q	C	H
U	R	G	E	L	S	H	T	I	U	J	V	K	W	S	X	L	V	Y	M	C	Z	N	O	E	A	N	R	B	P	B
N	Q	L	R	E	R	K	S	J	T	I	U	H	V	G	W	F	I	X	E	N	Y	D	Z	S	A	D	U	B	C	R
T	M	Y	S	T	J	O	H	N	R	I	V	E	R	N	O	P	L	Q	S	E	R	I	T	M	U	W	B	V	X	E
A	Z	A	N	B	O	C	P	D	Q	E	R	F	S	G	T	H	L	I	U	R	J	N	K	E	L	V	S	M	W	A
I	N	F	C	A	R	A	Q	U	E	T	O	E	P	D	Q	C	A	R	B	W	A	G	Z	N	S	Y	I	T	X	D
N	G	M	H	L	I	K	J	J	K	I	L	H	M	G	N	F	G	O	E	A	P	D	Q	C	R	B	R	S	A	T
S	T	A	G	E	C	O	A	C	H	C	R	B	S	A	T	Z	E	U	Y	L	V	X	W	W	X	V	R	Y	U	Z
D	Q	E	P	F	O	G	N	H	M	I	L	J	K	K	J	L	I	M	H	T	N	G	O	F	P	E	O	Q	D	R
U	P	P	E	R	C	A	N	A	D	A	V	I	L	L	A	G	E	X	W	S	Y	V	Z	U	A	T	M	B	S	C

1. ____________________
2. ____________________
3. ____________________
4. ____________________
5. ____________________
6. ____________________
7. ____________________
8. ____________________
9. ____________________
10. ____________________
11. ____________________
12. ____________________
13. ____________________
14. ____________________
15. ____________________
16. ____________________
17. ____________________
18. ____________________
19. ____________________
20. ____________________

Famous Canadian Lighthouses

The first lighthouses were burning bonfires located on the ends of points of land at harbour entrances. Later, these lights were replaced by towers with fire beacons on the top. Candles, oil lamps, and eventually kerosene lamps were used as beacons in the early 1800's.

Cape Spear Lighthouse

The lighthouse at **Cape Spear**, Newfoundland has flashed its message to ships and mariners since the mid 1800's. The original building was a square, two-storey structure with the light tower itself in the middle of it. In September 1836, the light was in operation and in 1878, a fog horn was added to guide ships into St. John's Harbour.

The first light came from another lighthouse in Scotland. The light rays came from seven burners and were intensified by curved reflectors. The lamps and reflectors were held on a metal frame which rotated slowly to produce a seventeen second flash of light, followed by forty-three seconds of darkness. The movement of the light was controlled by a clock-like mechanism. The light underwent many changes down through the years and in 1930, it was operated by electricity.

During the Second World War, Cape Spear became a coastal defence battery, equipped with two fifteen centimetre guns to be used to protect the entrance to St. John's Harbour from German submarines and raiders off the coast of the Island. The guns were built at the tip of Cape Spear and were connected by underground passageways to the magazine (storage for ammunition) and equipment rooms. Troops were stationed here from 1941-1945 and barracks, mess halls, and canteens were built. At the end of the war, most of the buildings were demolished except for the gun emplacements which remind us of a sombre period in our military history.

Today, Cape Spear Lighthouse has been restored to its original appearance and refurnished as a lightkeeper's residence to the period of 1839. The bunkers and the gun barrels provide an excellent view of the ocean where visitors search the horizon for whales, icebergs, seabirds and ships heading in and out of the St. John's Harbour. The Cape Spear Lighthouse is the oldest surviving lighthouse on Newfoundland.

Sambro Island Lighthouse

The **Sambro Island Lighthouse** is the oldest operating lighthouse in North America. It is located on Sambro Island in Halifax Harbour, Nova Scotia. It was constructed of stone in the years 1758-1759 and stood eighteen metres high from the base to the vane on top of the rocky island, 21.6 metres above sea level with a fixed light.

Often the light was not lit and ships entering the harbour would have to fire their canons to announce their arrival in order for the lighthouse keeper to light the lamp. Fog also caused serious problems for ships and mariners and some type of fog signal was needed on the Island. A signal station was built and manned by three men of the Royal Artillery. During a fog, ships would fire a shot to notify the lighthouse of their presence. The Royal Artillery would respond with two shots in quick succession.

Over the years a variety of fog horns and steam whistles were tried but they failed the test until 1972, when two fog horns were established at Sambro Island. In 1968, a simple airport rotating beacon was placed inside the top of the lighthouse.

Today, Sambro Island Lighthouse is still in use and is unmanned. Its light guided General Wolfe out of Halifax Harbour on his way to conquering New France in 1759. The Sambro Island Lighthouse was the last North American building seen by thousands of Allied navymen on their way to the First and Second World Wars.

Race Rocks Lighthouse

The **Race Rocks Lighthouse** is the oldest, manned lighthouse in Western Canada. It is situated on Vancouver Island, southwest of Victoria, in British Columbia. It was built in 1860 by the British and the crown colony on Vancouver Island due to the increase of maritime traffic bringing immigrants seeking their fortunes in the gold rush.

The Race Rocks Lighthouse was built of granite block construction which makes its appearance unique and rare in comparison with the other lighthouses found in Canada. The lighthouse towers 31.5 metres ending at its circular glass light. There were many dangerous areas to navigate through the Esquimalt Sound in the Straits of Juan de Fuca. Many ships were wrecked in the dangerous riptides around Race Rocks.

Cap-des-Rosiers

Cap-des-Rosiers is the highest lighthouse in Canada standing 33.6 metres. It stands on the Gaspé Peninsula in Québec. The shores of this large area are sprinkled with many reefs where storms and fog caused many ships to wreck against the Forillon Rocks or the coast of Cap-des-Rosiers in the early days.

Steamship owners pressured the colonial government to improve a system of navigational aids for the colony's major commercial waterway especially after the loss of the steamship 'The Canadian' that sank below Québec City in 1857.

The Cap-des-Rosiers Lighthouse is a 28.5 metre, nine-storey high tower measuring 7.5 metres in diameter at the base tapering to five metres in diameter at the lantern gallery. The limestone walls are 2.1 metres thick at the base and .9 metres thick at the top. The large lantern sits at the summit and the original burner used whale and porpoise oil until 1868, when coal oil was substituted. A spiral staircase runs the height of the 3.3 metre wide interior space.

Lighthouses are buildings that evoke romantic feelings, thus poetry, stories, books, and songs have been written about them. The sights and sounds they have seen and heard would provide a writer with many a historical tale.

Name: ____________________

Lighthouse Word Study

Read the information entitled Famous Canadian Lighthouses.

Match the words written in the box to their meanings. Record each word on the line provided.

1. ______________________ a fuel-oil obtained from petroleum or coal
2. ______________________ a place to store arms, ammunition and provisions for use in war
3. ______________________ pull down or destroy a building
4. ______________________ highest point; top
5. ______________________ unusual, having no like or equal
6. ______________________ signal light; guide or warning
7. ______________________ a building
8. ______________________ parts of a machine
9. ______________________ seaman, captain of a merchant ship
10. ______________________ to make or become stronger
11. ______________________ buildings used to lodge military men
12. ______________________ a meeting place for soldiers on a military camp
13. ______________________ soldiers; armed forces
14. ______________________ dark, gloomy, dismal
15. ______________________ platforms for guns
16. ______________________ belonging to the past
17. ______________________ artillery unit of guns, men and vehicles
18. ______________________ strong surface currents from shore

summit	**riptides**	**unique**	**sombre**	**emplacements**
demolish	**barracks**	**canteen**	**magazine**	**troops**
mechanism	**battery**	**kerosene**	**mariner**	**beacon**
structure	**intensified**	**historical**		

Famous Canadian Canal Systems

The early settlers and explorers discovered that Canada had an abundance of freshwater rivers and lakes. They used these waterways as highways for travelling and transporting their goods from place to place. The numerous sets of rapids and waterfalls were often obstacles around which they had to portage and which delayed their travelling time. Eventually, canals were built making the waterways navigable mainly for military defence.

The first canal system built was the **Rideau Canal** by Lieutenant Colonel John By, a British engineer. It is the oldest continuously operated canal system that connects Kingston to Ottawa. The building began in 1826 and the work was completed by hand. Hundreds of Irish, French Canadians, British labourers and stonemasons battled the Canadian wilderness, the working conditions, and malaria to complete this canal system in less than six years. In 1832, one of the greatest engineering feats was finished producing one of North America's best navigable waterways.

One of the engineering triumphs of the Rideau Canal is the beautiful arched dam at Jones Fall and the four locks. The dam was one of the first of its kind and the highest in North America. It is 105 metres wide and 18.6 metres high making it the largest such structure in the world.

Although the Rideau Canal system was built for defence and had forts, towers, blockhouses, and settlements of trained loyal settlers along its navigable waters, it was never used as a military supply route.

Today, the Rideau Canal system is a popular vacation spot for boating, cruising, recreation, fishing, tourism, enjoying the outdoors and appreciating our Canadian heritage. The locks along the Rideau River are still hand-operated at most of the twenty-four lockstations. The system is one hundred and sixty-eight years old and covers 202 kilometres from Kingston to Ottawa.

The **Trent-Severn Canal System** links Lake Ontario at Trenton with Lake Huron at Port Severn on Georgian Bay. The waterway is 388 kilometres long using the Trent to Rice Lake, the Otonabee River, the Kawartha Lakes, channels to Lake Simcoe and Lake Couchiching and the Severn River to Georgian Bay as well as two marine railways at Big Chute. At Peterborough and Kirkfield are hydraulic lift-locks unique to North America.

The **Trent-Severn Waterway** was a dream that took eighty-seven years to build before it became a reality. It began at Bobcageon by settlers who were anxious to have a waterway that would provide them access to southern markets. In 1833, the first wooden lock was built. Work on the waterway was sporadic until 1878 when Sir John A. Macdonald's newly elected government promised to complete the canal. Locks were built at Burleigh Falls, Lovesick, Buckhorn, and Fenelon Falls between 1883 to 1887. The Kawartha Lakes finally became navigable from Lakefield to Balsam Lake. Construction on the waterway continued until 1920 when the entire system was finally fit for travelling.

The Trent-Severn Canal system's recreational use began early. During the 1800's, Rice Lake, Lake Simcoe and the Kawarthas were used for regattas, fish and game clubs and conservation associations. During the 19th century, steamboats and railways carried vacationers to summer resorts that were opening up throughout the Kawarthas such as in Lakefield and Lindsay. This was known as the 'golden age' of steamboating and vacationing resorts on the Kawarthas. It was a time of steamboat excursions, huge regattas, bonfires, dances, marshmallow roasts, and picnics. The events brought crowds from all over dressed in formal attire, wide-brimmed hats and colourful parasols.

The invention of the gasoline engine, the automobile and improved roads ended the age of the steamboat and its whistle that announced guests were arriving. Today, the Trent-Severn Canal system is extensively used by boaters and cottagers.

The **Welland Canal System** has been built four times. Each time it was built, many improvements were made to accommodate the evolution of the North American shipping trade during the past one hundred and sixty years. It is a

navigational canal that is 43.5 kilometres long crossing the Niagara Peninsula of Southwestern Ontario. It connects Port Weller on Lake Ontario with Port Colborne on Lake Erie. The canal overcomes a height difference of 99.4 metres between the two lakes and bypasses the turbulent Niagara River and Niagara Falls.

During the fourth building of the Welland Canal, the locks were built wider, longer and deeper to accommodate larger ships. The number of locks were reduced as well which reduced a ship's travelling time through the canal.

The **Sault Ste. Marie Canal System** was built between 1889 and 1895 to bypass the dangerous rapids of the St. Mary's River and to provide the last link in Canada's Great Lakes-St. Lawrence shipping route. The construction of the canal was very challenging. It had to be cut through the bedrock of St. Mary's Island. The lock chamber was 274 metres long and 18 metres wide and was one of the world's largest.

For four years, stone cutters laboured building the lock chamber out of limestone and the approach walls out of sandstone. The canal had many advanced features and 'firsts' of waterway engineering technology. The watering and dewatering system decreased the turbulence during filling and emptying by allowing the water to flow through the lock floor. The gates and valves are operated electrically controlling the flow of water into and out of the new lock.

From the 1890's to the 1960's, schooners, steam-driven passenger ships, coal freighters, and private yachts have been locked through the canal. In 1979, the canal was retired from the St. Lawrence Seaway system and used for pleasure craft. In 1987, due to a structural failure, the lock was closed for eleven years and in 1998, it was reconstructed as a recreational lock and opened to boat traffic.

Activity

Name: ______________________

Name That Canal!

Read the information on famous Canadian canal systems.

Record the name of the canal system that answers each question on the line provided.

Rideau Canal	Welland Canal	Trent-Severn Canal	Sault Ste Marie Canal

1. Which canal system took eighty-seven years to build?
____
2. Which canal system was closed for eleven years and then reopened?
____
3. Which canal system was built four times?
____
4. Which canal system had to be cut through the bedrock of an island?
____
5. Which canal system has two hydraulic lift-locks and two marine railways?
____
6. Which canal system was built by Lieutenant Colonel John By?
____
7. Which canal system is 388 kilometres long?
____
8. Which canal system was completely dug by hand by hundreds of workers?
____
9. Which canal system was built to bypass the Niagara River and Niagara Falls?
____
10. Which canal system has the largest lock chamber?
____
11. Which canal system had steamboats taking vacationers to summer resorts and on short excursions?
____
12. Which canal system was built to protect the early settlers from invading forces?
____
13. Which canal system was made larger to accommodate larger lake freighters?
____
14. Which canal system was the first one to be built?
____
15. Which canal system has twenty-four lockstations that are operated by hand?
____

Name: ____________________

Canada's National Heritage Sites

Parks Canada is responsible for Canada's program of commemorating historical sites, people, and events. The most common form of commemoration is by a plaque or a simple marker. There are many historical sites located throughout Canada.

Using your favourite internet search engine search for "National Heritage Sites of Canada".

Click on a site that you wish to investigate.

Find out the following information:

1. What is the name of the heritage site that you visited?

   ____

2. Where is the heritage site located?

   ____

   ____

3. What special events take place at the site?

   ____

   ____

   ____

   ____

   ____

4. Why is this heritage site important?

   ____

   ____

   ____

   ____

5. When is the heritage site open?

   ____

6. How much does it cost to visit it?

   ____

Acitivity

Name: ____________________

National Landmarks of Canada

Using the internet or an encyclopedia, find the location of the following landmarks.

National Landmark	Location
1. Hawthorne Cottage	
2. Red Bay	
3. Queenston Heights	
4. Bar U Ranch	
5. Alexander Graham Bell	
6. Fisgard Lighthouse	
7. Grand Pré	
8. Province House	
9. York Factory	
10. S.S. Klondike	
11. Ryan Premises	
12. Sainte-Anne-de-Bellevue Canal	
13. St. Andrews Blockhouse	
14. Saint-Louis Mission	

Name: ____________________

Canada's Natural Wonders

Mother Nature has created many amazing natural wonders in Canada. Some of these wonders are described below. Research to find out in which province each one is located. Record your answer on the line provided.

1. **Long Beach** is located in Pacific Rim National Park. It is an eleven kilometre curve of sand pounded by the surf backed by a dense rainforest and high mountains. ____________________
2. **Lake Louise** is the most famous, the most visited, and the most photographed lake in Canada. ____________________
3. **Percé Rock** is a huge reddish-gold rock that rises like a giant ship just off-shore from the town of Percé. ____________________
4. **Gros Morne National Park** provides tourists and hikers with the most spectacular scenery in eastern Canada. ____________________
5. The **Badlands** was once the home of large dinosaurs and the region is filled with fossils. It is an eroded valley of the Red Deer River where cactus grows.

   ____
6. The **Paint Pots** are found near the Vermillion River. They are three pools containing so much iron that their clays are stained red, yellow, and orange. First Nations peoples used the ochre clay to decorate themselves, their teepees, and their clothing. ____________________
7. Over the years the powerful Bay of Fundy tides have sculpted the red cliffs at Hopewell Cape into strange rocky, giant, tree-crowned islands that look like **flower pots** when the tide is out. ____________________
8. The **Maligne Canyon** is the most spectacular and longest of the many gorges seen in the Rockies. ____________________
9. **Niagara Falls** is one of the wonders of the world. You can stand at the brink and watch the water plunge over the edge. ____________________
10. At **Magnetic Hill**, an optical illusion makes cars appear to coast uphill with the motor tuned off. ____________________
11. **Takakkaw Falls** is one of the highest waterfalls in Canada. It is over seven times higher than Niagara Falls. A huge jet of water pours over the edge of a sheer cliff and drops in two stages to the valley floor. ____________________
12. In **Cathedral Grove** you may walk under giant Douglas firs. The largest ones are eight hundred years old and rise to sixty metres or more.

    ____

Activity

Designing a Landmark Pamphlet

Most landmarks are written about in pamphlets and brochures and given out at tourist bureaus to visiting tourists.

Choose a landmark that is found in your province or territory.

Research the landmark and find out the following facts:

Library of Parliament

What? What is it?
What material was used to make it?

Where? In which province or territory is it found?
In what city or near what city, is it?

Why? Why is the landmark located there?
Why would tourists or visitors want to visit it?

CN Tower

Who? Who built the landmark?
Who can use it?
Whom does it represent?

How? How does one get to it?
How was it constructed?
How many does it hold?
How much does it cost to visit?

When? When was the landmark built?
When is it open to the public (times, seasons)?
when in history did the event it represent take place?

After you have collected the necessary information, create a pamphlet about the landmark.

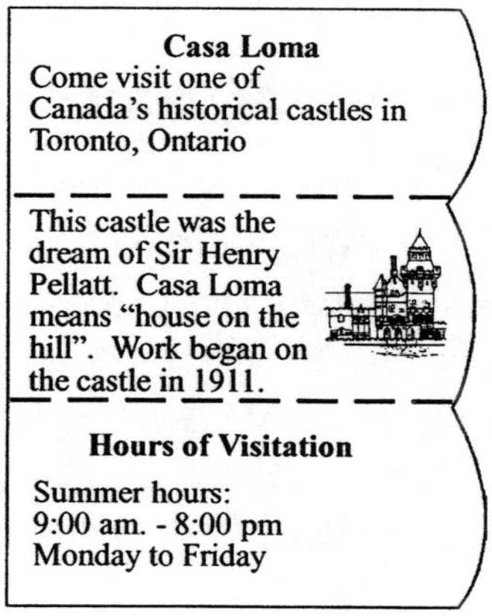

The Peace Bridge

Answer Key

Let's Research Canada's Capital Region!: (page 7)

1. There are thirteen statues.
2. Sir John A. Macdonald; William Lyon Mackenzie King; Sir George-Étienne Cartier; Queen Victoria; Lester B. Pearson; John G. Diefenbaker; Alexander Mackenzie; George Brown; Thomas D'Arcy McGee; Robert baldwin/Sir Louis-Hippolyte Lafontaine; Queen Elizabeth II; Sir Wilfred Laurier; Sir Robert Borden
3. Answers will vary.
4. There are ten monuments.
5. a) The Canadian Tribute to Human Rights - Corner of Elgin and Lisgar Streets
   b) The Terry Fox Statue - 90 Wellington Street
   c) National War Memorial - Confederation Square
   d) The Peacekeeping Monument - Sussex Drive, corner of St. Patrick Street
   e) Anishinabe Scout - was located below Champlain Monument
   f) The Commonwealth Air Force Memorial - Gree Island, across from Ottawa City Hall
   g) Never Again War Monument to Peace and Remembrance - near St. Joseph Boulevard and Alexandré - Taché Boulevard in Hull
   h) The Colonel By Monument - Major's Hill Park, Ottawa
   i) Champlain Monument - Nepean Point, Ottawa
   j) The Tomb of the Unknown Soldier - in front of the National War Memorial

Ottawa's History Challenge: (page 8)

5, 10, 14, 1, 7, 18, 2, 6, 3, 8, 12, 9, 17, 11, 15, 13, 16, 4

The Parliament Buildings: (page 12)

1. **A.** Parliamentary Library **B.** Centre Block **C.** East Block **D.** Centennial Flame **E.** West Block **F.** Peace Tower
2. Answers may vary. Possible Answers: Canadian flag, maple leaf, Canadian Coat of Arms , maple tree, maple syrup, beaver, Canadian money, Bluenose Schooner, CN Tower, Bonhomme, moose, polar bear, totem pole, Royal Canadian Mounted Police
3. **a**) Centre Block **b**) East Block **c**) West Block **d**) Centre Block **e**) House of Commons **f**) The Senate Chamber **g**) Centre Block **h**) The Senate **i**) Parliamentary Library **j**) Peace Tower **k**) House of Commons **l**) The Senate Chamber **m**) Parliamentary Library
4. Answers will vary.

Parliament Hill: (page 16)

1. They represent democracy, freedom of speech, tolerance, good citizenship, and determination.
2. They are called the Centre Block, the East Block, and the West Block.
3. They are examples of High Victorian Gothic architecture.
4. a) a curved structure capable of bearing the weight of the material above
   b) a support built against a wall or building to strengthen it
   c) a projection or ornament on the outside of a building

d) odd or unnatural in shape or appearance

5. The House of Commons and the Senate Chamber are found in the Centre Block.
6. The Peace Tower was built and dedicated to the more than 60 000 soldiers who died during World War One.
7. The Summer Pavilion was rebuilt to honour police officers killed in the line of duty.
8. The statues were erected to honour famous Canadians who helped build Canada.
9. The Centennial Flame represents Canada's unity.
10. Answers will vary.

Discover the Parliament Hill Statues: (page 21)

1. 5 Lester B. Pearson
2. 10 Robert Baldwin, Sir Louis-Hippolyte Lafontaine
3. 2 William Lyon Mackenzie King
4. 1 Sir John A. Macdonald
5. 6 John G. Diefenbaker
6. 4 Queen Victoria
7. 12 Sir Wilfred Laurier
8. 9 Thomas D'Arcy McGee
9. 3 Sir George-Étienne Cartier
10. 7 Alexander Mackenzie
11. 11 Queen Elizabeth II
12. 8 George Brown
13. 13 Sir Robert Borden
14. 1 Sir John A. Macdonald
15. 2 William Lyon Mackenzie King
16. 12 Sir Wilfrid Laurier
17. 11 Queen Elizabeth II
18. 1 Sir John A. Macdonald, 3 Sir George-Étienne Cartier

Can You Name Ottawa's Official Residences?: (page 26)

1. Stornaway **2.** 24 Sussex Drive **3.** The Farm **4.** Rideau Hall **5.** Stornoway **6.** The Farm **7.** 7 Rideau Gate **8.** Rideau Hall **9.** 24 Sussex Drive **10.** Rideau Gate **11.** The Farm **12.** Stornoway **13.** Rideau Hall **14.** 24 Sussex Drive **15.** Rideau Hall **16.** Answers will vary.

Research a Monument: (page 30) - Answers will vary.

Where Would You Find It?: (page 36)

Part A:

1. (3) **2.** (5) **3.** (1) **4.** (6) **5.** (4) **6.** (7) **7.** (8) **8.** (9) **9.** (6) **10.** (1) **11.** (3) **12.** (5) **13.** (6) **14.** (7) **15.** (8) **16.** (9) **17.** (10) **18.** (1) **19.** (10) **20.** (9)

Part B: Answers will vary.

When Did It Happen?: (page 41)

1. 1870 **2.** 1713 **3.** 1948 **4.** during the War of 1812 **5.** 1930 **6.** 1719 **7.** between 1832 and 1837 **8.** during World War One **9.** 1961 **10.** 1758 **11.** August 1936 **12.** World War Two

Let's Use the Internet!: (page 42) - Answers will vary.

Name That Castle!: (page 45)

1. Craigdarroch Castle **2.** Dundurn Castle **3.** Casa Loma **4.** Dundurn Castle
5. Casa Loma **6.** Craigdarroch Castle **7.** Dundurn Castle **8.** Dundurn Castle
9. Craigdarroch Castle **10.** Casa Loma **11.** Craigdarroch Castle **12.** Casa Loma
13. Craigdarroch Castle **14.** Casa Loma **15.** Dundurn Castle

Canada's Historic Homes: (page 50)

Part A:
1. Oshawa, Ontario **2.** Victoria, British Columbia **3.** Dawson City, Yukon
4. Prince Edward Island National Park **5.** Kingston, Ontario **6.** South St. Vital, Manitoba

Part B:
1. Parkwood Estate **2.** Bellevue House **3.** Green Gables **4.** The House of All Sorts
5. Robert Service Cabin **6.** Riel House **7.** Bellevue House **8.** Parkwood Estate
9. Green Gables **10.** Riel House **11.** Parkwood Estate

Famous Canadian Bridges: (page 54)

1. False **2.** True **3.** False **4.** True **5.** False **6.** True **7.** False **8.** False **9.** True **10.** False
11. False **12.** True **13.** True **14.** False **15.** True

Canadian Towers Crossword Puzzle: (page 58)

Heritage Word Search: (page 63)

C	A	R	I	B	O	O	W	A	G	O	N	T	R	A	I	L	Z	Y	R	H	E	R	I	T	A	G	E	F	C	S
A	S	R	N	A	Q	V	P	N	W	O	X	O	N	Y	M	Z	L	A	K	B	J	B	C	A	M	T	R	H	G	O
R	T	U	T	R	O	U	N	T	M	T	L	W	K	C	J	R	A	I	S	H	G	K	C	F	T	E	I	U	D	U
I	P	V	E	K	Q	B	R	I	S	H	I	S	T	O	R	I	C	E	A	R	Z	I	D	Y	X	C	W	D	V	R
B	X	U	R	E	S	R	Q	Q	P	T	O	C	N	S	M	L	A	F	K	E	G	N	H	E	I	F	J	G	H	D
O	V	Y	P	R	W	Z	A	U	P	B	O	O	C	T	D	N	D	E	M	V	F	G	G	T	H	L	I	K	J	O
O	Q	C	R	V	R	D	S	E	T	E	U	W	V	U	W	F	I	X	G	I	Y	S	H	R	Z	A	I	B	J	U
M	X	N	E	I	V	Y	U	Z	T	A	S	B	R	M	C	Q	A	D	P	R	O	L	N	A	M	E	L	F	K	G
O	G	H	T	L	I	M	U	S	E	U	M	J	F	E	K	E	N	L	D	E	M	A	N	D	O	P	G	Q	C	H
U	R	G	E	L	S	H	T	I	U	J	V	K	W	S	X	L	V	Y	M	C	Z	N	O	E	A	N	R	B	P	B
N	Q	L	R	E	R	K	S	J	T	I	U	H	V	G	W	F	I	X	E	N	Y	D	Z	S	A	D	U	B	C	R
T	M	Y	S	T	J	O	H	N	R	I	V	E	R	N	O	P	L	Q	S	E	R	I	T	M	U	W	B	V	X	E
A	Z	A	N	B	O	C	P	D	Q	E	R	F	S	G	T	H	L	I	U	R	J	N	K	E	L	V	S	M	W	A
I	N	F	C	A	R	A	Q	U	E	T	O	E	P	D	Q	C	A	R	B	W	A	G	Z	N	S	Y	I	T	X	D
N	G	M	H	L	I	K	J	J	K	I	L	H	M	G	N	F	G	O	E	A	P	D	Q	C	R	B	R	S	A	T
S	T	A	G	E	C	O	A	C	H	C	R	B	S	A	T	Z	E	U	Y	L	V	X	W	W	X	V	R	Y	U	Z
D	Q	E	P	F	O	G	N	H	M	I	L	J	K	K	J	L	I	M	H	T	N	G	O	F	P	E	O	Q	D	R
U	P	P	E	R	C	A	N	A	D	A	V	I	L	L	A	G	E	X	W	S	Y	V	Z	U	A	T	M	B	S	C

Words To be Found:

Caribo Wagon Trail, Cariboo Mountains, St John River, St. Lawrence River, Caraquet, Morrisburg, antique, tow scow, stage coach, sourdough bread, costumes, tradesmen, museum, interpreters, historic, heritage, Kings Landing, Acadian Village, Barkerville, Upper Canada Village

Lighthouse Word Study: (page 67)

1. kerosene **2.** magazine **3.** demolish **4.** summit **5.** unique **6.** beacon **7.** structure **8.** mechanism **9.** mariner **10.** intensified **11.** barracks **12.** canteen **13.** troops **14.** sombre **15.** emplacements **16.** historical **17.** battery **18.** riptides

Name That Canal!: (page 71)

1. Trent-Severn Canal **2.** Sault Ste. Marie Canal **3.** Welland Canal **4.** Sault Ste Marie Canal **5.** Trent-Severn Canal **6.** Rideau Canal **7.** Trent-Severn Canal **8.** Rideau Canal **9.** Welland Canal **10.** Sault Ste Marie Canal **11.** Trent-Severn Canal **12.** Rideau Canal **13.** Welland Canal **14.** Rideau Canal **15.** Rideau Canal

National Landmarks of Canada: **(page 73)**

1. Brigus, Newfoundland **2.** Newfoundland **3.** Niagara-on-the-Lake, Ontario
4. Near Longview in Alberta **5.** Baddeck, Nova Scotia **6.** Near Victoria, British Columbia **7.** Near Wolfville, Nova Scotia **8.** Charlottetown, Prince Edward Island
9. Churchill, Manitoba **10.** Hwitehorse, Yukon **11.** Bonavista, Newfoundland
12. West Montréal, Québec **13.** St Andrews, New Brunswick **14.** Honey Harbour, Ontario

Canada's Natural Wonders: **(page 74)**

1. British Columbia **2.** Alberta **3.** Québec **4.** Newfoundland **5.** Alberta
6. British Columbia **7.** New Brunswick **8.** Alberta **9.** Ontario **10.** New Brunswick
11. British Columbia **12.** British Columbia